# Miata
# MX·5 GUIDE

Jay William Lamm

Motorbooks International
Publishers & Wholesalers

First published in 1990 by Motorbooks International Publishers & Wholesalers, P O Box 2, 729 Prospect Avenue, Osceola, WI 54020 USA

The information in this book is true and complete to the best of our knowledge. All recommendations are made without any guarantee on the part of the author or publisher, who also disclaim any liability incurred in connection with the use of this data or specific details

Motorbooks International books are also available at discounts in bulk quantity for industrial or sales-promotional use. For details write to Special Sales Manager at the Publisher's address

Library of Congress Cataloging-in-Publication Data
Lamm, Jay William.
    Miata MX–5 Guide / Jay William Lamm.
      p.   cm.
    ISBN 0-87938-466-2
    1. Miata automobile.   I. Title.
TL215.M45L36   1990         90–5914
629.222'2—dc20              CIP

Printed and bound in Hong Kong through Bookbuilders, Ltd.

**On the front cover:** *A brilliant blue Miata MX–5 on a brilliant day of sunshine and open, winding roads. This is what the Miata is all about.*

**On the back cover:** *The screaming yellow show car Miata Club Sport Racer, an example of what could come from Mazda or what the Miata enthusiast could construct at home. Performance springs and anti-roll bars from Jackson Racing's MazdaSports. Another view of the Club Sport, complete with aftermarket Momo steering wheel.*

**On the frontispiece:** *The Racing Beat customized Miata MX–5. This Anaheim, California, company has dominated IMSA GTU racing with its RX–7, and has now turned its hand to the MX–5.* **Racing Beat**

**On the title pages:** *Rural sports car turned city slicker. With a little help from Rod Millen Motorsports, the Miata cuts a debonair figure against the Los Angeles skyline.* **Guy Spangenberg**

**On the contents page:** *Diamond Head, Hawaii, and the Mazda Miata MX–5.*

*To Robert and Charlie*

I would like to thank the following for their invaluable assistance in preparing this book:
Fred Aikins, Mike Allen, Barbara Beach, Peter Bohr, Duane Bowen, Dave Brownell, John Butler, Rod Bymaster, Teresa Cameron, Michael Dregni, Pete Drexler, J. Michael Farber, Peter Farrell, Elizabeth Gardiner, Norman Garrett III, Neil Griffin, Matthew Hall, Harry Hayashi, Hill & Knowlton, Toshihiko Hirai, Michael Hohn, Ellen Houston, International Motor Sports Association, Mark Jordan, Judy Kaufman, Wayne Killen, Ed Kjar, Sandy Kocsis, Mary LaBarre, John Lamm, Michael Lamm, Robert Lamm, Gary LaPlant, Alex Maduros, Rob Maintowel, Yasao Maruta, Mazda Corporation, Mazda Motor of America, Jim Mederer, Miata Club of America, Timothy Moy, Tetsuo (Ted) Nagase, Al Nimmo, Brett O'Brien, Steve Parker, Karen Penn, Steve Potter, Bob Richards, DeeDee Rowe, Alan Shaffer, Mike Sharp, Simpson Brothers Racing, Duane Simpson, Tom Smitham, Dave Solar, Sports Car Club of America, Vincent Sweeney, Jonathon Thompson, Vince Tidwell, Sonny Tippe, Peter Vance, Peter Vance Studios, Lyn Vogel, Washington Automotive Press Association, Greg Woo, Jack Yamaguchi.

# Contents

# The Appeal of Open Sports Cars

Some people—a lot of people—say there's no accounting for the appeal of small, open sports cars. They think you simply have to appreciate them firsthand to understand. I used to be one of these people myself. The first car I ever owned was a 1959 Triumph TR–3, and all my farm-bound buddies in rural California were discovering Camaros, Mustangs and Barracudas at the time. Despite their raised eyebrows, there was an emotional tug too strong to resist from cars like the TR. I couldn't explain it, but I knew I felt it.

That red-orange Triumph, despite being what I'd call a beater today, remains one of my favorite cars of all time—and that's an opinion I think is only a little colored by nostalgia. My TR was completely honest: it delivered exactly the handling (extreme power oversteer), performance (dog slow) and reliability (precious little) that I expected. When I first looked at the car I knew exactly what I had: a classic sports car, for better or worse. The designers knew it, too. There were three ways to start the engine; usually you used a button in the cockpit. When that didn't work,

there was another button under the hood. And when *that* conked out, there was a crank you could use to turn the engine over by hand.

I had to use that crank many times, and the fact that I continued to love the car dearly made me believe that my affection for the TR was too irrational to be explained—it simply defied logic.

My next car was a chrome-bumper MGB roadster, another completely illogical choice. After looking at lots of reliable and brutally fast American iron, that butterscotch MG was the only car that moved me in the least. I bought it, drove it for four years and loved every minute of it—except maybe the time the fuel pump went out eight miles down a dirt road on Memorial Day.

After the MG, I knew that no matter what my friends said, I was going to continue my sports car affair. One day I went out and test drove a Lotus Elan Series IV roadster, top down, big-valve engine, Gold Leaf Team Lotus paint. Lord, that was a beautiful car! The Lotus was tiny, clean and *fast*; it made the MG seem huge and ponderous. The Elan was a direct

connection to the road, and I sensed I'd found the essential British sports car. When the electrical system melted down ten miles later, I knew I'd been right.

I didn't buy the Lotus, and I kicked myself about that right up until the day I saw the first Mazda MX–5 Miata photo in *Autoweek*. With a single glimpse of the Miata, I made a stunning realization—the emotional tug of my treasured British cars wasn't put there by invisible trolls who lived under the bridges of the Sussex countryside. It was put there by enthusiasts like me, designers and engineers who simply knew that driving a car should be more than an exercise in transportation. Those enthusiasts could be Japanese and American just as easily as English.

A car, they knew, was a personality with which you should have an ongoing, splendid rapport. A companion that's not only willing to come along for the ride, but eager as all get-out to make it a good time. Mazda knew this all along with the Miata. They took a clean sheet of paper and set out to rediscover what made the driver and car fuse into one.

British sports cars are certainly companionable, but they're also a mite cantankerous. They're the sort of friends who are known to complain and moan now and then, and ruin some trips in the process. That means that only people who are willing to forgive their friends from time to time—I must be one, I suppose—can ever love them. Japanese cars used to be the other way around, stone reliable cold fish. I also owned a 280Z, and though that car would run rings around any of my English cars I never came close to feeling the same sort of affection for it.

With the Miata I suddenly saw a fusing of the best of both worlds: a car as fun as any MG and as trustworthy as a Mazda. The Mazda will no doubt do to British sports cars what Honda did twenty years ago to British

motorcycles—make them seem a little silly. And if MG and Triumph weren't already dead, the Mazda Miata would kill them off as surely as the Honda 750 killed Norton and BSA.

The impression that Japanese cars would always sacrifice soul for reliability made most enthusiasts think there would never be a true Japanese sports car, and we knew that our own beloved brands would never survive the era of Japanese-defined quality. Sports cars seemed to be a dying breed. We had gained excellent transportation, we thought, but lost

our dearest friends . . .

    . . . until the first time we saw a Miata. The true, honest, open, low-cost, legitimate, classic sports car had returned, and it was going to be reliable to boot. When I got to drive my first MX–5, all my happiest suspicions were confirmed. Mazda had built exactly the sort of car that we had all thought we'd never see again.

    What a revelation that day was!

*Jay William Lamm*
*January 1990*

*Triumph's TR–2/TR–3 was the classic 1950s sports car: plebian underpinnings, light weight, low cost, exciting styling.* **Mark Terrapelli**

# CHAPTER ONE

# The Miata's Concept and Heritage

Before you can really appreciate the coup that Mazda's pulled off with the MX–5 Miata, you must have answers to some basic questions about sports cars. What are they? Where did they come from? How did America come to appreciate them? And, since Mazda has proven with the Miata that a sizable market still exists for classic examples, why did they disappear from our shores for almost a decade?

### The sports car tradition

Defining the term sports car has always been a knotty problem. To one person, a three-door Acura Integra with power windows might qualify; to another, nothing less than a roofless, doorless Lotus Seven will do.

By the broadest definition, a sports car is any vehicle designed with driving pleasure first and foremost in mind. But as your definition narrows, a sports car comes to be described by omission. It's a vehicle minus all components that are unnecessary for pleasurable driving; a sacrifice to lower weight and the performance and handling benefits that come with it. Extra seats, extraneous luggage

capacity and extra size eliminate many cars from the classification.

Defining a sports car has become harder over the years. At first, all cars were basically playthings for the wealthy, and as such they probably all fit the sports car classification. But as time went on and cars became legitimate tools of transportation, those designed strictly for enjoyment began to carve out their own niches. Soon afterward, even more specialized cars appeared that were suited only for racing. Before World War II, racing cars were most often legitimate road-going cars as well.

The definition came to mean a vehicle that served that dual purpose: It could be driven over regular roads with more or less satisfaction during the week, then modified slightly for racing on the weekend. The romantic image of the sports car was one in which the owner, almost always a man of means, would bomb around town looking for a scratch race or just getting to where he was going. On the weekends it was assumed he would remove his fenders, muffler and headlights and head off to a legitimate racetrack to compete. Cars as diverse as the Aston Martin, Bentley, Bugatti, Duesenberg, Stutz, Delahaye and Alfa Romeo typified the breed.

Throughout the 1930s, however, racing cars continued to become more specialized toward while larger companies continued to build such vehicles more for their engineering and publicity benefits than overall profits. The market for inexpensive open sports cars continued to grow in Europe in the years leading

*Arguably the most significant sports car of all time, the MG TC introduced affordable sports cars to the vast American market.* **Lamm-Morada Publishing**

competition only, and soon many of them were no longer legitimate street machines. The dual-purpose definition remained with sports cars, while the overall performance title shifted to pure racing cars in the Formula classes. A new breed of sports car appeared *en masse* to fill the widening gap between everyday transportation and racing car. These were typically small, light, open cars using many proprietary components like drivetrains and suspensions from more sedate family machines, and they began to offer entertaining driving for the more budget conscious.

The best and most famous examples came from England in the form of the MG and Riley, and to a lesser extent Frazer-Nash and Triumph. Sports cars became the livelihood of these manufacturers,

up to World War II, but it was still a small one overall.

The Second World War brought a new element to the European sports car scene: Americans. Yanks who couldn't fulfill their romantic impulses by piloting P–51s and B–17s could at least compensate with the slower but generally less dangerous business of driving sports cars. Sports cars were a new pleasure for most Americans, and many took to them grandly.

When the war ended the Yanks returned home, often bringing an MG

*The MGB entered the market in 1962 and didn't leave for 28 years. Almost a half-million MGBs made it onto the road, most of them in North America.* **Mark Terrapelli**

*The epitome of middle-ground sports cars, the Austin-Healey 3000 slotted nicely between MG and Jaguar in price, performance and status.* **Lamm-Morada Publishing**

with them, and introduced the affordable modern sports car to America. Their influence would result in the birth of the largest sports car market the world has ever known: North America. By 1950 about 5,000 sports cars, many of them in MG's renowned TC series, were being sold in the United States. That was against a backdrop of millions of vehicles overall, but sports cars gained a lion's share of the publicity and prestige in those days. By 1955, Ford and Chevrolet were offering open two-seaters of their own while Triumph, MG, Austin-Healey and Jaguar had built thriving businesses out of such cars.

It was a time of tremendous excitement and diversity in the market. At the top end, the Jaguar XK–120 and 140, Mercedes 300SL and Chevrolet Corvette V–8 offered performance equal or nearly equal to the fastest two-seater racing cars of the day. At the lower end, MG, Triumph and Porsche were pushing relatively inexpensive and thoroughly enjoyable machines that could be afforded by great numbers of people.

The market continued to thrive throughout the 1960s, with selections filling every income and performance niche. Ferrari, Mercedes-Benz and Maserati offered blindingly fast and expensive sports cars for the rich, while Triumph, Fiat and MG advanced the state of the lower end to a fine art. In between came Alfa Romeo, Austin-Healey, Jaguar and a few others. The sports car market was reaching what many would later consider to be its peak.

As different as a Ferrari 250 GTO might have been from a Triumph Spitfire Mark II, both were readily identifiable as sports cars. They were both front-engine, rear-drive two-seaters that compromised very little indeed to comfort and convenience over pure driving entertainment. But a movement was afoot since the mid

*Though it aged better than the MGB, the Fiat 124/2000 Spider was pretty long in the tooth by 1980. Once the Japanese arrived in force it never held more than a token share of the sports car market.* **Lamm-Morada Publishing**

1950s that would eventually make the sports car definition a tough, if not for a time impossible, one.

This was the move to grand touring, or GT, cars: cars that offered nearly or as much performance as sports cars, while throwing in a healthy dose of creature comforts as well. These could be as closely related to traditional sports cars as mere coupe forms of recognized convertible sports models: the MGA Fixed Head Coupe and Mercedes 300SL Gullwing, for example. Or they could be coupes and even sedans built by recognized sports car makers, like Aston Martin's DB series, Ferrari's four-place 250 and 330 GTs, Jensen's Interceptor and the Lamborghini Espada. Or they could even be, as the 1960s went on, relatively inexpensive and wholly un-sports-car-like in appearance, such as BMW and Alfa four-doors.

When the day came along that a BMW sedan could easily outrun a traditional sports car like the MGB, the sports car definition became as murky as a London fog. Obviously the MG

was a sports car and the Bimmer was not, but anything in between became increasingly difficult to identify.

GTs didn't play havoc only with the sports cars' definition—they played havoc with their sales as well. Eventually they got much of the credit or blame for driving traditional sports cars from the market.

### America, Japan and the days before Miata

Still, it wasn't all that long ago when Americans had a large field of traditional sports cars to choose from. It was 1970 when MG offered the MGB and Midget, Triumph had the TR-6, GT-6 and Spitfire, and the Italians offered up Spiders from Alfa and Fiat. Sunbeam was hanging on by

13

its toes and the defunct Austin-Healey 3000 could still be had as a leftover on new-car lots. Lotus would happily sell a Seven or Elan to anyone willing to pay the price, in both money and convenience, and even Nissan, née Datsun, offered the 2000, a car that unknowingly presaged a revolution two decades later: the Mazda MX–5 Miata. At the top end of the market, Ferrari had a small number of Daytona Spyders to offer, Maserati the Ghibli roadster, Jaguar the open V–12 E-Type and Chevrolet the Corvette convertible.

Car enthusiasts love to discuss the slew of events that led to the demise of the traditional open sports car. They'll say that tightening smog and safety regulations in the 1970s did them in. Or that they suffered when gas prices soared and America's love of automobiles went sour. Or that the less expensive examples got passed up in performance and reliability by GTs from Europe and Japan.

All true enough, these things were really just symptoms of a bigger problem. The manufacturers of that era's inexpensive sports cars either

*Fiat's mid-engined X1/9 promised to be the hottest lightweight sports car of the 1970s, but sluggish acceleration and spotty build quality kept it from being a big success.*
**Lamm-Morada Publishing**

could not, or would not, adapt to new expectations. Eventually the romantic lure of their products couldn't sway enough buyers from the concrete advantages of the opposition to keep the companies solvent.

Another big nail in their coffin was the revolutionary 240Z. The Datsun 240Z offered superb performance, style and reliability at about the same price as the competition's older models, and it *ran*. No oil leaks, no goofing around; it just *worked*. The Z was an instant success.

And while the Z kept getting better through the decade, European sports cars born in the 1960s became more emasculated and troublesome. The venerable MGB, once one of the best all-around sports cars available to the masses, became heavier, slower, uglier, taller, terminally plastic-ridden

At the top of the market, the Europeans generally abandoned open sports cars for two-place coupes and mid-engined GTs. In America, the Corvette became saddled with smog equipment, and the convertible disappeared from the line-up in 1976 due to buyer ennui. The traditional sports car seemed dead, though Triumph, MG, Alfa Romeo and Fiat refused for a time to hear the news.

and less reliable while the Z gained fuel injection, a five-speed transmission, a string of luxury options and a growing list of converts. In a strictly rational sense, the Z car was vastly superior to anything the British or Italians could offer at twice the price. Even in the emotional sense—the one that sold sports cars—it was a force to be reckoned with.

*Datsun/Nissan's Z car defined a new standard for low-cost sports cars. By 1975 it had fuel injection, a luxurious interior and the best per-dollar performance on the market.* **Mark Terrapelli**

15

Onto this stage a new player arrived at the end of the decade. With traditional sports cars in decline and the Z car reaching more fans every year, a second Japanese manufacturer arrived with their own iteration of the new breed of sports cars: Mazda's RX-7. The RX-7 was a completely new animal. The first thing you noticed was its styling: clean, smooth and elegant where the Z car was growing fat and covered in gewgaws. The second was the engine.

even if buyers were still not convinced of the engine's longevity they fell in love with its performance. The RX-7's rotary was small, light, made gobs of silky power and revved like a 750 motorcycle. (It proved, incidentally, to be tough as nails as well.) The RX-7 gamble paid off, and buyers came back to Mazda with a newfound love.

Through most of the 1980s, the RX-7 was perhaps the purest sports car Americans could buy on a reasonably small budget. Its

*The larger, heavier, more luxurious and faster RX-7 works perfectly with Mazda's 13B rotary. The light and basic LWS would have been another matter.* **Mazda**

Mazda's earlier rotary-powered cars took it on the chin when reliability and fuel consumption woes surfaced in the mid 1970s: pinning their hopes on another Wankel-powered car was a tremendous gamble. But in the RX-7,

competition was the Datsun Z, Toyota Supra, Chevy Corvette, Porsche 924 and 944, and some Johnny-come-latelies like the Pontiac Fiero and Toyota MR2. (Somewhere off on the sidelines were the Alfa Spider and Fiat's 2000 and X1/9—never really contenders and happy to get what little pie they could.)

Of all the cars in the big-sales league it competed with, the RX-7 was always the cleanest, most honest and most obviously a true sports car. It never apologized for being a machine that was designed mainly for fun, and for that it was the first choice of a whole lot of buyers.

Mazda is something of a wild card in Japanese auto making. Toyotas seem to be designed by researching a market to find a need; Hondas reflect a cold and intensely analytical approach to auto making. But Mazda's offerings always appear to have been conceived first in the soul. And while the company's engineers can certainly take a passionate concept and turn it into a remarkably functional package, that touch of soul somehow remains intact. This is the proper way to design a sports car, and it's how the RX-7 came to hold the position it has for more than a decade.

For all that, the RX-7 was never a *traditional* sports car. It was always a sophisticated, high-tech tool for going fast. Many owners had no idea or even interest in how the engine worked— just that it did. Traditional sports cars, at least to Americans, had always been something else: simple, easily understood convertibles that weren't necessarily fast but only had to *feel* that way.

Like many of the great cars in this world, the RX-7 should not have been built, nor the MX-5 Miata. It's hard to believe that either car, both tremendous gambles when seen on a sheet of paper, made it past the finance staff and number crunchers that constitute any car company's conscience.

But, that both cars proved tremendous commercial successes once they made it into production isn't surprising at all. Both were built *by* enthusiasts *for* enthusiasts, and that whole process defies the bean-counters' logic. There was no hard evidence that buyers would go for a rotary sports car in 1978, and good evidence that they would not. There were no figures showing that a traditional, open, straightforward

sports car would sell like gangbusters ten years later, either. The car fans inside Mazda knew better both times. They knew that if you made a car that was good enough and fun enough and affordable enough, people would appear from beyond the market surveys to snap it up.

## Early stirrings

Robert (Bob) Hall was the West Coast stringer for *Automotive News* in 1979, and its enthusiast-based sister magazine *AutoWeek*. In that capacity he

*Raised in a house full of sports cars, Bob Hall went from journalist to product planner just in time to shepherd the Mazda Miata into production.* **Mazda**

found himself in Hiroshima, Japan, chatting amiably with an elderly gentleman about cars, their mutual favorite subject. His fellow enthusiast was Kenichi Yamamoto, Mazda's managing director and later simply The Boss.

The conversation naturally turned to the sorts of cars that Hall thought Mazda should build in the future. Yamamoto wasn't just making small talk—he knew how valuable the thoughts of other enthusiasts could be.

No doubt conversations like this one had led to the RX-7 that was just then proving so successful.

Bob Hall had an answer already framed in his excellent Japanese. "A low-priced, open-bodied sports car," he suggested without hesitating. As the conversation heated up, Hall even sketched out the idea on a nearby blackboard, as though Yamamoto needed a visual cue to stick the thought in his mind. Hall didn't know it at the time, but he'd just laid the groundwork for a big piece of his life. Two years later, he'd join Mazda's North American arm and get a chance to make his chalk drawing come to life.

## Offline, Go, Go

In 1978, Mazda reincarnated itself with the RX-7 and quickly re-established itself as a full member of Japan's auto making club. Soon after, a strong family tree evolved with solid, successful branches, including the 323 economy model, the 626 mid-size, the big 929, the RX-7 sports car, a line of pickup trucks and some commercial vehicles. All of them were respected and profitable.

For most companies, that kind of comeback would be cause for celebration, but Mazda's upper management didn't see it like that. To them, it was almost a hazard. Mazda was built on qualities like daring, innovation and enthusiasm, and those qualities set the company and its buyers apart from the rest of the Japanese auto scene. With material success came a very real danger of Mazda losing its forward-thinking identity, both in the marketplace and the engineering studio.

Michinori Yamanouchi, then responsible for Mazda's product planning and development, set out to keep the company looking ahead. He put together a program in November of 1983 with the purpose of simply looking into the future—playing with

new cars, new ideas and new markets that might (or might not) pan out someday. In Japanese fashion, the program was given an odd yet somehow appealing name: Offline, Go, Go.

Offline, Go, Go kicked around all sorts of entertaining ideas, its small group of engineers blue-skying like kids discussing what they wanted for Christmas. They talked about off-road sports cars, pocket-sized racers and

*Some distinct Miata character is beginning to show in this early Mazda North America (MANA) sketch: the wide stance, short length and pinched "Coke bottle" sides.* **Mazda**

other pie-in-the-sky projects that they'd personally love to work on. Their most common desire was also the one that happened to have the most chance of ever becoming a production model—a lightweight sports car, or LWS as they called it. Bob Hall and Kenichi Yamamoto weren't the only ones who'd thought about reviving the dying market.

So Offline, Go, Go settled on an LWS as the outlet for its considerable energy. In retrospect, it was

imagination, and as such discouraged learned advice from the company's finance staff.

As an advanced concept and little more, Yamanouchi knew that Offline, Go, Go's LWS activities could exist unchallenged for a while. But he also suspected that if the time came to think about building such a car, an LWS might have strong support in Mazda's atypically car-crazy upper management, especially from Yamamoto. He turned the fledgling

*What many people thought was gone forever: top down, country road, sunny day, tach at six grand.* **Mazda**

presumptuous to even suppose that Mazda could build three different sports cars in one decade—two generations of RX-7 and then the LWS. But then production still wasn't the real goal of Offline, Go, Go. It was simply an exercise to stretch Mazda's

program over to a talented advanced concept engineer, Masakatsu Kato, and made it legitimate with the project number P729.

But the P729 wasn't going to stay solely at Mazda's Hiroshima headquarters for long. Mazda, like many other Japanese companies, had recently finished establishing an American arm, Mazda North America (MANA). The new southern California-based division included a Product Planning and Research (PP&R)

staff complete with stylists, a fact that would have a profound effect on the progress of the LWS.

Yamanouchi and Kato decided that work on their latest sports car should be carried on simultaneously in Japan and at MANA. There were three ways to build their LWS, they realized, and they might as well let MANA pursue one of them.

**Front/front, front/rear or mid/rear**

A modern car company that wants to build an affordable LWS can go about it three ways. Since they probably have a small front-wheel-drive car in production, they can do what Honda did with the CRX and go for a front-engine/front-wheel-drive (called an FF) layout. There are many advantages to going this route, the most important being that the car almost builds itself from existing parts. The prohibitively expensive process of tooling up to build new components is largely avoided. All the manufacturer has to do is take their bread-and-butter front-drive chassis, hop it up and maybe shorten it and drop on a slick two-seater body. The result: instant sports car. And, as the Honda CRX proved, quite possibly a very good one.

Another option would be to emulate high-dollar exotics and race cars and go for a mid-engined, rear-drive (MR) design. This wouldn't be as difficult as it sounds—an existing front-drive powertrain can easily be moved to the back of a car and used as a mid-engine unit. Such a car would cost more than an FF, because it would need many more original pieces, but buyers might be willing to pay more in the end because of the exotic allure of its mid-ship engine. (Toyota and Pontiac were actually going ahead and doing this while Mazda thought about it, and they came up with the MR2 and Fiero, respectively.)

Finally, a company could build a sports car the way it used to be done, with a front engine driving the rear

*Toyota went the MR (mid-engine, rear-drive) route for their lightweight sports car, the MR2. The Miata would have been much the same if management had opted for a mid-engined design.* **Lamm-Morada Publishing**

*The FF (front-engine, front-drive) sports car layout was most successful in Honda's CRX Si. Existing front-drive components saved Honda money, but the cost was front-drive handling.* **Lamm-Morada Publishing**

wheels (FR). For a company like Mazda with no small FR cars in production, there were no monetary advantages to this kind of layout. There's also less interior room in an FR than in an FF of equal size, and engineers are able to make all but the fastest FFs corner just as quickly as a similar FR.

There are plenty of advantages to FR, though, that have nothing to do with overall cornering speeds or economics. First and foremost, a front-driver can never *feel* like a rear-driver. It might indeed corner just as quickly, but it won't feel nearly as good doing it. Front-wheel-drive cars seem to have a mind of their own, and getting them around a curving mountain road can often be more work than fun. A light, powerful rear-driver, on the other hand, is an increasingly rare and sweet pleasure. The driver can control the direction of the front end with the steering wheel or the rear end with the throttle, and the car communicates its intentions much more pleasantly.

Another advantage to the front-engine/rear-drive scheme is simple tradition. It's the layout traditional sports car people grew up with, the sort they remember fondly and know how to drive. This was a particularly important consideration if Mazda intended to give buyers back the kind of lightweight sports cars that had just disappeared, a key idea from the beginning. Many company insiders felt that buyers should be able to recognize a lightweight sports car as being just that, and FR would be a big help.

**Competition for P729**

With all these alternatives to work out, Mazda installed a thoughtful-looking designer named Yoichi Sato in a tiny Tokyo design studio and told him to oversee Japan's two proposals into the LWS project. Meanwhile at MANA, Shigenori Fukuda would oversee the American effort.

Sato would pursue the MR and FF variants, which was fine with

*From left: Norman Garrett III, Miata concept engineer; Shinzo Kubo, Miata project manager; and Shigenori Fukuda, Mazda design chief.*

Fukuda. For the MANA contingent, nothing but the FR would do—in fact, nothing but an FR *convertible* would do. MANA's designers and engineers were dead-set on interpreting the lightweight sports car in its most traditional sense.

MANA's layout engineer at the time, Norman Garrett III, recalled the feeling: "I wrote a searing epistle as to why it had to be FR. And I really believed it would be done. Inside Mazda you really started to believe that there's a philosophy of not doing cars just for profit, but doing cars for progress. Are we going to show that we're just here to make money, or are we here to make good cars?'

"We pulled out all our guns propaganda-wise, trying to convince Mazda that if it was a front-wheel-drive everyone would say, 'Aw, it's just a convertible 323,' whereas if it were rear-wheel-drive it would show that we were a premier sports car maker. Front-wheel-drive—and this was my statement—is chosen to optimize interior packaging, and a sports car has no business optimizing interior packaging [at the expense of performance]. It has no interior packaging; just two seats. And if you make a two-seat car front-wheel-drive, you're just showing that you're trying to save money by using an off-the-shelf drivetrain and powerplant."

The MANA team had considerable talent to put toward the task. Fukuda and his assistant, Masao Yagi, were both well-proven designers, while a young American of good styling stock named Mark Jordan would also be working on the car. Jordan had come to MANA after proving himself at GM-Opel in Germany. Another team member was also fresh from a German tour, this one at BMW: Tsutomu (Tom) Matano. Bob Hall would also be around to keep tabs on "his" project, and Norman Garrett was put into the effort to backstop the designers. Garrett, in

other words, would make sure that what the team was proposing could actually be done.

Still, Mark Jordan, for one, was far from convinced that MANA's FR proposal would be triumphant: "The Japanese . . . were looking at new, new, new all the time, and cars like the CRX were really making a splash—and the Fiero." Also, he remembers, "In the early stages of the game I thought it was going to be difficult to convince them [Mazda's home office] of FR, because from a financial standpoint the front-drive unit already existed from

*The surface becomes smoothed out on MANA model number one. At this point, auto design leaves the business of sketching and painting and becomes one of sculpture.* **Mazda**

the 323. It would have been very easy to take that unit and stick it in a sporty car." Jordan intentionally uses the word sporty in place of sports. "The thing was, there were a lot of things from a design stance that we didn't like with front drive, the first being a high cowl (windshield base). But I was afraid that the front-drive would probably win just from a financial standpoint."

## The LWS steps closer to reality

Competing programs progressed on both sides of the ocean until April 1984, when Mazda held the first official viewing of all three proposals *in vitro*. Fukuda, Jordan, Hall and Kubo escorted sketches of MANA's FR to Hiroshima, where they were presented alongside Sato's MR and FF efforts. (They didn't know it, but the MR program was already on the way out. A layout engineer in Sato's group, Masaaki Watanabe, had assembled a

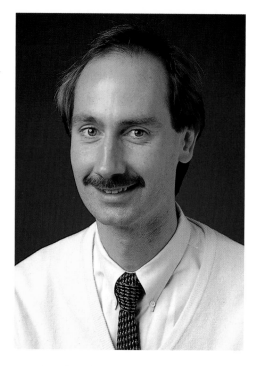

*Mark Jordan, fresh from a stint in Germany at General Motors' Opel organization, would be with the Miata from start to finish.* **Mazda**

testbed MR with less-than-promising results.)

MANA's FR sketches didn't give the Japanese designers any reason to worry—in fact, they felt rather sorry for Fukuda's people, who seemed to have come all the way to Japan for nothing. The head of the Tokyo team viewed the California-penned roadster as merely nice, not great, and no big threat to his own proposals.

As Mark Jordan saw it, "Our sketches unfortunately didn't capture at that time the animated personality that makes the Miata stand out, so in that respect their sketches were better than ours—just the sketch *style* was better. They really worked hard, and they had pretty interesting-looking, strong-impact sketches on the wall. And sometimes it doesn't matter how good a concept is, if you can't sell management with sketching then sometimes you lose." Yoichi Sato, the leader of the Japanese design team, was beginning to feel confident.

Four months later Sato's opinion changed dramatically. When the time came to show full-scale models, under Masao Yagi the MANA FR proposal had become a sleek, exciting shape while neither of the Tokyo cars went anywhere. The Tokyo studio offered up a front-engined car along the lines of the later Buick Reatta and a mid-engine package smacking of Pontiac's Fiero. "Androgynous," Bob Hall later labeled them.

MANA's open roadster, however, was something else entirely; their stylists had literally carved out a vivid and exciting sports car concept. "We really shaped a lot of it by hand," Mark Jordan remembers, "just kind of letting our feelings come out through the clay tool. Usually the modeler takes a designer's sketch, but in this case the designers just got in there and started feeling for the shape."

The result was a friendly, outgoing, *instantly recognizable* sports car, and that's what MANA's presentation

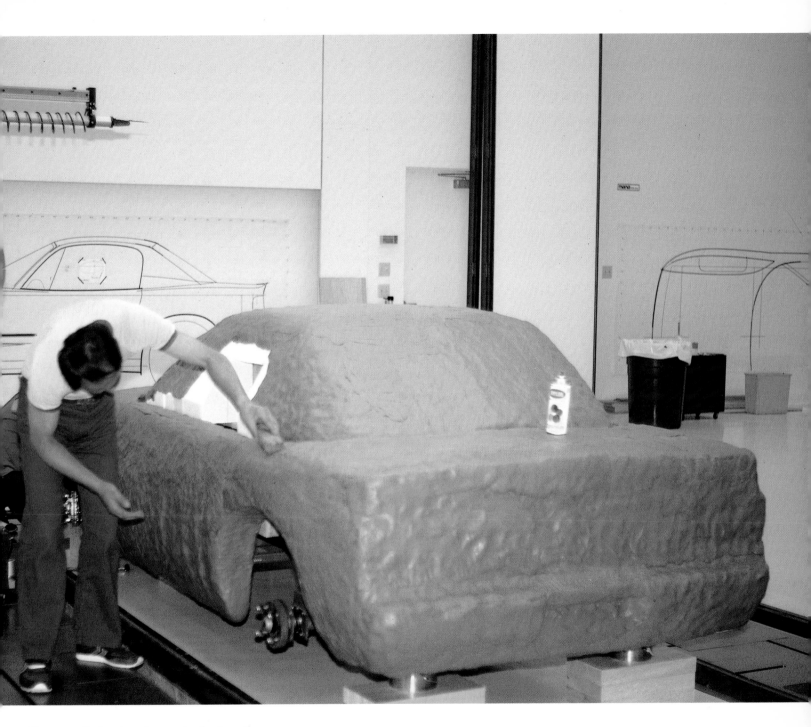

*Clay was piled on top of a wooden buck as the first step in building MANA's original LWS model. The modeler then painstakingly carved out the shape envisioned by designers.*
**Mazda**

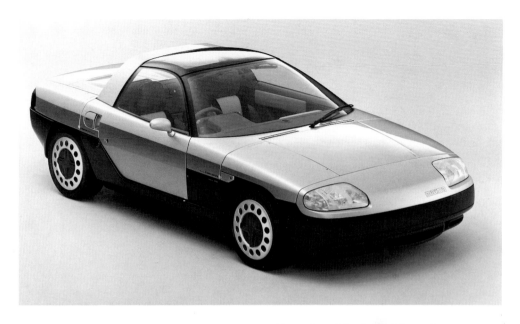

*For a time, Mazda's MX-04 show car competed with the P729 for time and money at Mazda's Technical Research Center.* **Mazda**

*The MX-04 featured modular bodywork, a concept that Mazda strongly believes in for the future. This is the same MX-04 in roadster form.* **Mazda**

hit upon over and over. Their proposal, Fukuda said, was not a sporty car, or a sports coupe or any other offering that had to be qualified. It was a sports car, plain and simple, and anyone looking at it would know that right away.

MANA had hit on an important point. Nobody really knew what cars like the CRX and Fiero *were*—were they sports cars? Economy cars? Who could tell? The roadster from California, however, left no doubt whatsoever. From the open top to the rounded front and rear ends, the car pushed all the right sports car buttons.

MANA continued to pitch, and the arguments in favor of FR continued to mount. Their car would *feel* like a sports car, because it had rear-wheel-drive. It would attract many buyers for no other reason than its convertible top—open sports cars had been gone for about five years, just long enough for Americans to start missing them. Employment would rise significantly in the sunbelt states by 1990. The reasons to go with MANA's classic design were legion, at least to hear Shigenori Fukuda and his staff tell the story. "And," adds Jordan, "I think Bob Hall did a good enough job telling them that [FF] wasn't going to do it—that we shouldn't even bother building something like that."

Sato and his team were left in stunned, if gracious, defeat. There was simply no coming back from MANA's onslaught. Even those who'd worked hard on the competing proposals came away convinced that an open-bodied, front-engined, rear-drive sports car was the way to go.

## Getting P729 on the road

With official acceptance of MANA's concept as the right one for P729, Masakatsu Kato had to move fast. If he wanted Mazda's LWS to be more than an enjoyable design exercise (and did he ever!), he'd have to get things moving immediately. Soon after the front-engine/rear-drive layout was chosen, a meeting took place in

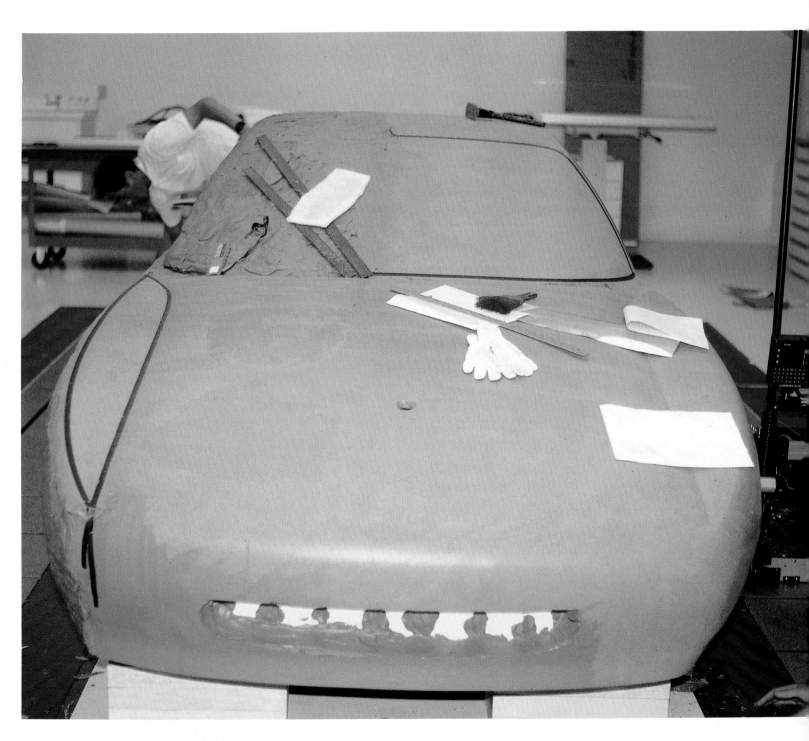

*Subtle curves like fenderlines weren't fully described by designers' sketches for the first MANA model: the designers went in and carved them out in three dimensions.* **Mazda**

Hiroshima that determined how such a car should be built.

Entering the picture were Takao Kajima, Mazda's resident suspension wizard, and development engineer Hirotaka Tachibana. These two men would later prove essential to the final form of the car. Along with Masaaki Watanabe and Norman Garrett, they set down some important layout elements, particularly the exact engine location, and many would remain with the car until it saw production.

The entire P729 program—including project head Kato—was shifted over to Mazda's brand-new Technical Research Center soon thereafter. Kato continued working on the myriad details and then delegated the project to an unexpected place: England. While the work went on there, neither Hiroshima nor California would have much to do with Mazda's LWS.

**The British connection**

In the Sussex coast town of Worthing, England, John Shute had just been handed responsibility for the next big step in Mazda's development of the P729. Shute, a former GM-Vauxhall body engineer, was the owner of International Automotive Design, Europe's largest independent engineering and design company.

Kato sent the project out for a number of reasons, most notably the fact that his operation and MANA's had other things to work on. There was Mark Jordan's design for a 323 convertible to be dealt with—an almost certain production model—and the MX-04 dream car which would see the light of day at auto shows around the world. Simple economics constituted another factor: technically, the strong yen would buy more work from Shute's IAD employees than Mazda's own.

From MANA's first clay model, IAD put together a running prototype with the experimental code number V705. The V705 was cobbled up from various bits of Mazda running gear and IAD's own imagination. A plastic body with a central backbone frame, à la Lotus, was assembled around a futuristic interior based on MANA sketches. It might have been a one-off, but the V705 was completely functional, down to and including a cigarette lighter.

*MANA's roadster would have looked silly without an interior, so one was carved to fill the space in the first clay model.* **Mazda**

*Hardtop boot, with and without semi-faired headrests, was often bandied about by MANA but never saw factory production.* **Mazda**

For hardware, IAD borrowed three different sets of used parts. A secondhand GLC wagon gave its engine and transmission to the cause, while the front suspension came off an old RX-7. The rear trailing arms were 929 parts. It was an inelegant solution, but more than effective enough to do the job.

**American exposure**

The original plan was to take IAD's cobbled-up prototype and ship it straight to Japan for official review. But Masataka Matsui, head of Mazda's new Technical Research Center, had a better idea. Matsui figured that since America was the car's biggest intended market, it should go to America and be judged first in its natural environment.

Norman Garrett was put in charge of the outing. "Mr. Matsui," he remembers, "had this wonderful philosophy of wanting to see a car in traffic before he would say whether it was going to be good or not. A static clay model is a very dangerous thing to build a car on. The V705 prototype was built to show how the [car's styling and concept] would or wouldn't work. I don't think we learned so much from an engineering standpoint, because the package was all wrong: The car could never be built that way. You could

29

hand-make the car, but you could never mass-produce it."

Arrangements were made to ship the V705 to the scenic beach town of Santa Barbara, California. MANA and Matsui made an outing of it, taking along the V705, an RX-7, a Honda CRX that had been turned into a convertible and MANA's own white Triumph Spitfire. Anyone who's ever spent the day tooling around Santa

*As the "Yagi model" LWS shape became cleaner and more defined, character lines finally were added to bring it to life.* **Mazda**

Barbara's warm, beautiful streets will know how pleasant such an assignment could have been, but for Norman Garrett, at least, it wasn't all fun and games.

"We were worried about spy photos, but we weren't so smart as to take off [our California] distributor

license plate, which everybody in the world knew belonged to Mazda. We unloaded the thing off the truck, and we couldn't find the key. And it's sitting there in the wide open, and I was the guy who drove it off the truck, so I'm feeling pretty stupid. And then these guys started to show up with cameras. . . . Anyway, it was the same mistake I make with my Miata now—the key was in the trunk lock.

"It was dangerous, but boy, Matsui got some neat opportunities to see the car; to see the public go wild about it. There's a Porsche/Rolls-Royce dealership at the corner of State Street and Highway One, and I pulled up to that intersection and got stuck at a light—I was really paranoid about being stuck at lights because of photographs. Anyway, I looked over at the showroom. There was a new Porsche 930 slopenose in it and a lot of yuppies hanging around, and one by one they came to the window. Everybody came to the window and started staring at the Miata! There was a [Mercedes] Gullwing and some other classics in the showroom, and they weren't looking at those!"

Bob Hall, who'd recently come from the media himself, had similar worries. He agreed with Matsui's plan, but knew that a leaked photo now could botch the whole project before it officially started. Still, the chances of an enthusiast seeing the car, realizing what it was, having a camera nearby and knowing where to sell the photos were pretty slim. Hall's confidence held until the V705 drove up State Street past some familiar faces—the staff of *Road & Track* magazine eating lunch at an outdoor cafe. Jaws dropped on both sides of the windshield, and Hall had to read them the photo-leak riot act: "Publish one picture and you'll blow it for all of us. Leak the story and you'll never see this car in production!" (Much later a similar incident occurred when another automotive journalist was accidentally invited to participate in a Miata consumer clinic. The gravity of the situation was explained to this writer, too, and both viewings stayed secret.)

Matsui, meanwhile, was having a blast. People were chasing the V705 down the street to get a closer look at the car; the MANA driver was more willing to humor them. They were asking who built the roadster, what it was and where they could get one. Matsui must have known that such a

how the evening ended: "We left that restaurant, and we were walking through the parking lot. And this is the greatest moment in the Miata project to me: Matsui-san looked over and said to us, 'I think we should build this car.' That really was a turning point. Matsui had to be behind the project for it to go.

"The Santa Barbara trip was a risk well taken."

positive reaction from a random group of people was worth the results of twenty planned product clinics.

Hall, Fukuda, Garrett and the rest of the MANA team spent dinner that night discussing what Matsui had just seen, and Garrett vividly recalls

*To frustrate potential spy shots, Mazda dolled up an early road-going Miata in cloth "breadvan" bodywork.* **John Lamm**

*Engineer Norman Garrett III bought himself one of the first Miatas to reach the East Coast.* **Miata Club of America**

32

# CHAPTER TWO

# The Oneness Between Horse and Rider

By the end of 1985, MANA had built a second full-scale model to supersede the one they showed against the front- and mid-engined proposals from Japan. With the completion of model number two, the time had come to see if MANA was just wasting its time or on the way to building a real production car. Even though the LWS was still technically just a corporate muscle-stretch, considerable money and effort had gone into it by then. If any more resources would be sent its way, they had to be for a defined purpose.

So in early 1986 work began on a presentation specifically to plead for the P729's fate. Enthusiasts on both sides of the Pacific looked for solutions and benefits that would justify Mazda's continued support of the LWS project. They knew that strong financial factions inside the company had to be sold on the idea, even though most of Mazda's engineers and designers would like to see the LWS go full speed ahead. Cooler heads had to be convinced: even as powerful an ally as Kenichi Yamamoto, The Boss himself, wouldn't approve the car if it didn't seem likely to make at least a little money for the company.

Mazda is typically tight-lipped about the actual maneuvering that went on in deciding to upgrade the P729 from offline to online status. For the people at MANA, by the middle of 1986 the LWS *seemed* to be a go. "Sometime in mid '86 . . . they made the decision to go," remembers MANA designer Mark Jordan. "But even after that happened we had heard that it was still on shaky ground. It wasn't until the very end where it did get online and it was under full development." According to Jordan, at one time, while the company was not saying no to the project, it seemed it might get knocked out by another priority. "I think the management end was saying 'We've got to do the MPV [Mazda's sporty minivan], Light Sports will have to go on the back burner.' And we told them 'Forget the MPV, we're going to be the last ones on the market with that anyway. Let's do the Lightweight Sports, we'll be the first on the market.' They let us have both in the end," Jordan says.

Some insiders put the date of full corporate commitment much later: November 1987.

## Hirai to the fore

Whatever the P729's official status, Masakatsu Kato suddenly had a going concern on his hands. Kato inherited the Lightweight Sports Car and was overseeing it at the Technical Research Center, but when the P729 evolved beyond the TRC's jurisdiction, Kato had a decision to make. Would he stay with the LWS project and give up his work at the tech center, or vice versa? He chose to remain at the TRC working on advanced vehicles like the MX–04 show car. A new project leader had to be found for the P729.

Hirai, who'd followed the P729's progress with great interest, was ecstatic at his new assignment. But he knew it wouldn't be an easy task. Though the general look, layout and concept of the car had been settled on, there were literally thousands of problems still to be taken care of. What's more, Hirai knew that time was of the essence. Even though the P729 was officially a going program now, until a car is sitting on the showroom floor, all sorts of things can come along and kill it.

International Automotive

After considerable deliberation—men fought hard for a plum job like this—Mazda chose Toshihiko Hirai to take over the project. Hirai was formerly in charge of Mazda's breadwinner 323 line and had proven himself extremely capable. "Hirai really gets credit for being a man that rose to the occasion," Norman Garrett recalls, and no one at Mazda would argue with that.

*Mazda's MPV sport minivan competed with the LWS for funding and attention. Much to Mazda's credit, both projects eventually got the go-ahead.* **Mazda**

Design was brought back into the picture, this time to build mules (cobbled-up prototypes used to test basic ideas and parts). John Shute's IAD engineers were also given the task of building a number of vehicles based on the second MANA model.

Meanwhile, MANA's California crew was already working on their third and final full-sized clay. By this time the earlier team had been joined by Koichi Hayashi and Wu-Huang Chin. Chin, like Mark Jordan, was a recruit from GM-Opel. Chin deserves special credit for adding a crucial element to the design: the oval, organic theme that still holds the car together. The third model continued at an exciting pace.

Long gone by this time were basic questions of theme and detail. Fixed headlamps, for example, were long ago discarded for reasons of technology and possible public acceptability. The car would have a low, oval mouth, a character-giving bump on the hood and a clean, animated overall shape. Now came the difficult part—making it work.

Fortunately for Hirai's engineers and MANA's designers, many of the car's *hard points* were well known by then. Hard points are the basic dimensions that everyone has to work around—the wheelbase, engine height, seat position and so on. These had been looked at by Watanabe, Kajima, Tachibana, Garrett and others three years earlier, making everybody's job a lot easier.

During the first serious steps toward production, a lot of promising production programs fall apart when designers say they want one thing and the engineers want something else. The production team then has to come up with a compromise to solve the problem, and often that idea pleases no one.

The Japanese manage to avoid this for the most part because there's excellent communication—and plenty of mutual respect—between all the groups involved in building a car. It's not a matter of the designers versus the engineers versus the production experts, it's a team effort toward a common goal. If one group has a

problem in a certain area, the others don't consider it someone else's concern. They try to come up with common solutions.

It doesn't always work, though, and sometimes confrontations are inevitable. In the Miata's case such give-and-takes were avoided for the most part: the original hard point estimates were so good that everyone knew beforehand what they had to work with. As special problems were encountered—the cowl height (windshield base) was continually lowered, for example—they could be approached with evolutionary, rather than revolutionary, solutions.

This team philosophy was only part of what would make the Miata so special in the end. As Hirai remembers, the very *size* of the team was important, too: "This project was

standpoint, it was really hard to package. With the cowl height that the designers were fighting for, you really couldn't get a rotary in there. The centerline of a rotary engine is about four inches higher than the crankshaft center of a regular engine, so your bellhousing has to be four inches higher. And I'm glad, because a rotary just isn't the right engine for this car."

The decision was quickly made to go ahead with an inline four. Luckily, a big jump on the project had been accomplished already. One of the few LWS pieces to begin life in the corporate parts bin was its four-cylinder engine, which traces its roots to a high-output twin-cam used in performance versions of the 323. Mounted transversely, this engine—called B6–DOHC—was perfect for hot 323s. But it didn't perform the way the LWS engine was supposed to, so it was chosen only as a starting point. It would get a thorough going-over before seeing duty in the Miata's engine bay.

Under engine expert Kazuo Tominaga, the powerplant group already had decided what they wanted. The engine had to be light, of course. It had to have a rewarding amount of power, delivered in an exciting way. It had to look good when the hood was up, the way engines used to. And· finally, it had to be as reliable and well built as any other Mazda engine.

The first step was to remove as much weight as possible—no small feat since the B6–DOHC starting point was no pig itself. But some ingenious solutions lowered its weight even further. One of the best was a stainless-steel exhaust system, including an exotic stainless manifold of nearly equal tube lengths. The stainless system weighed thirty-nine pounds all told, about thirty percent less than a similar steel setup. (Stainless steel also won't rust and it sounds better than regular steel.)

Using smaller accessories also brought down the weight. A smaller fan motor, for example, could be fitted since the engine didn't need as much cooling when placed longitudinally instead of transversely. An aluminum block was about the only further step that could have been taken, but it was never even considered—no doubt its cost would have put the LWS's base price out of sight. The compact short-skirt cast-iron block of the 323 was a given.

The next concern was the engine's power and how it was delivered. Guaranteeing ample power would be relatively easy for Mazda's engine specialists, but tuning it properly was another matter. The actual delivery—that is, how the power comes on as the engine speed increases—was given tremendous thought. For the lightweight automobile at hand, it was decided to tune the engine in true sports car fashion: calm power at lower revs that climbed predictably to a wailing rush as the tach approached redline.

"When you get pressed into your seat on a runway in an airplane," explains Norman Garrett, "you get pressed into your seat and then it's pretty constant after that. What really makes a car feel fast is if acceleration is constantly increasing. With a rotary engine, the torque curve is very flat and the acceleration is very constant. You can get tremendous acceleration out of an RX–7 and blow the doors off most cars, but it doesn't *feel* as fast because your acceleration is constant. I was very key on requesting that however the final engine was tuned, the slope of the torque curve was such that we changed the acceleration constantly up to a very high rpm."

Traditionally, cars targeted for America have avoided this kind of tuning as Americans are notorious for under-revving their engines. But Mazda knew that in the 1980s that attitude had begun to change. Cars like the Honda CRX, Toyota MR2 and Mazda's own RX–7 had introduced high-winding engines to lots of

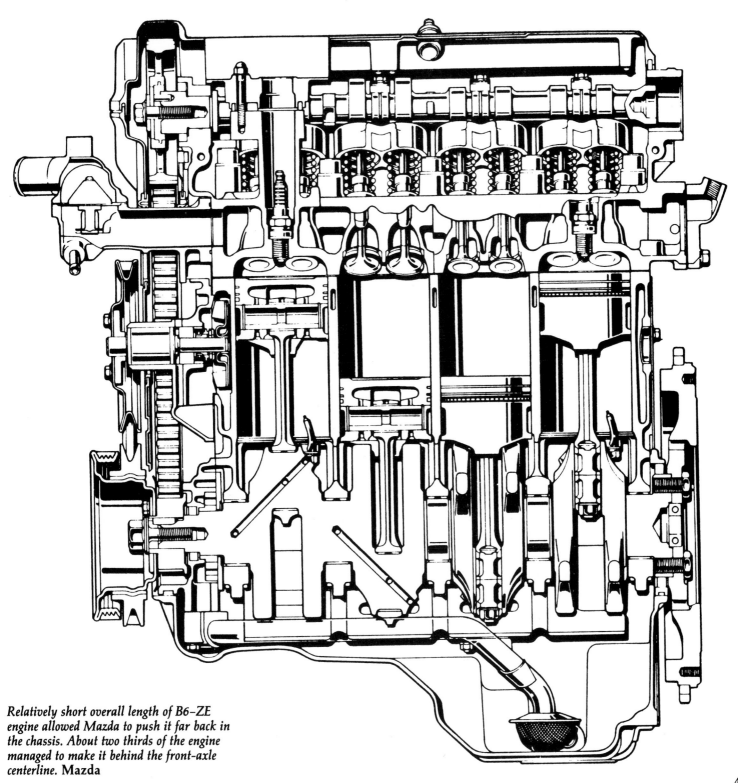

*Relatively short overall length of B6–ZE engine allowed Mazda to push it far back in the chassis. About two thirds of the engine managed to make it behind the front-axle centerline.* **Mazda**

47

Americans with good results. So the sports car fans who had previously experienced high-revving cars would already know how to use this engine, and the rest of the country had shown that it was able to learn.

To get the desired high-end behavior, Kazuo Tominaga and his engineering team looked to high-overlap, high-lift cams and huge intake and exhaust valves. The valves (their included angle was set at fifty degrees) were located in pentroof combustion chambers with central plugs; lift was 0.3 inches, and the intake and exhaust valves measured 1.22 and 1.03 inches, respectively. Given the engine's small size, this was a classic recipe for high-end power.

Feeding plenty of air and fuel into these deep-breathing combustion chambers would be a straightforward but highly developed fuel-injection system based on Bosch's L-Jetronic design. Tuned intake runners, each a relatively long 15.7 inches, again aided high-rpm performance.

The intake and exhaust systems were the brainchild of Tsunetoshi Yokukura, and when he was given the job he was immediately bombarded with questions. There was a strong group at Mazda that felt a multi-carburetor setup would be ideal for the engine, and they made some good arguments. Traditionally, big Weber-style carburetors are the stuff of which sports car dreams are made. Even today, an intelligently built multi-carb setup makes considerable power. Also, Yokukura was reminded, nothing would look quite as good as those big racy carbs perched nonchalantly on the side of the engine.

That was no small consideration. Remember that engine appearance was another one of the team's major goals. They'd already decided to go with an aluminum cam cover treated to look like a sand-cast piece, and great pains were being taken to make the engine compartment as clean and attractive as possible. The Miata would wind up

with one of the few engine bays in recent years in which the engine, not a tangle of wires and hoses, was the main focus.

But Yokukura, though he might have been tempted, found too many flaws with the idea of carburetors. Mostly he worried about the difficulty in getting them to perform decently after being saddled with American and Japanese emissions equipment. On their own, carburetors do a fine job of metering fuel and air to an engine, but in concert with anti-smog equipment they can be troublesome indeed. Carbs also require more maintenance than fuel injection, don't run as well in all temperatures and pressures and were quite frankly just too outdated. This sports car might have been inspired by the classics of the past, but it was going to be completely modern in its own right. Injection would be the way to go, Yokukura decided, and the results proved him right.

The exhaust system, as mentioned, was a lightweight stainless-steel tubular affair. Normally, only the most exotic and expensive sports cars use anything more than a simple cast-iron exhaust manifold and steel pipes. Not Mazda's P729. Taking weight, durability and sound into consideration, stainless seemed the only way to go. Yes, sound. The Miata was consciously designed to sound the way it does—its robust exhaust note isn't just the result of happy chance.

One of the things Japanese performance cars have often been criticized for is the sound of their exhaust. It seems at first a silly complaint, but sound is a large part of the driving environment. Exhaust noise helps the driver determine when to shift, lets him or her know how well the car is running and simply provides one more link between driver and automobile. And yes, a healthy exhaust note just *sounds good*.

Italian car companies have always known this, and they play to it. Jaguar and Lotus don't do too poorly either, and BMW hits a winner now and then. Japanese cars, however, are almost notorious for their lack of tailpipe music.

The principals of the LWS program were determined to make their sports car sound the part. Unlike the Italians, however, who seem to fiddle aimlessly until they get a sound they like, Mazda approached the problem in its typically analytical fashion. Hirai went so far as to make a tape of engines he particularly liked the sound of (more than 100 in all), and he played it time and again during his daily commute.

Makato Shinhama and a crew of young engineers spent long hours of overtime experimenting with pipes and mufflers until they came up with some excellent examples for their bosses to choose from. The choice for the exhaust note came down to two options, a light staccato rap or a heavier, throatier pulsing. Eventually, the throaty American-style bass was selected, the sound the car was introduced to the world with.

## Transmission and PPF

Rather than starting from scratch for the LWS transmission, Mazda knew that a development of the non-turbo RX-7's gearbox would fit the bill perfectly. But it wouldn't be a matter of simply dropping in the RX-7 unit. The transmission had to feel as tight and light as the car it would be used in. The small LWS would demand a different sort of transmission feel than the RX-7.

The RX-7 gearbox was by no means ponderous or heavy, but Mazda wanted the throws to be shorter and crisper still for the smaller car. Norman Garrett discussed transmissions at great length with his Japanese counterparts: "This was the famous quote of 'It should be a Jaguar E-Type crossed with a BMW 7-Series with a lot of miles on it.' You know, get the buttery feeling [of the BMW] and the solid clicks [of the Jaguar], and

keep the thing as short as you can." The distance between gears wound up being less than two inches, letting the driver shift simply with a flick of the wrist. Special detents were added to give gear changes a positive, mechanical feel.

New gear ratios were cut for the LWS, much more closely spaced than those in the RX-7, reflecting the four-cylinder's much narrower power band. Again, Garrett had a strong opinion on the design: "We were really trying to

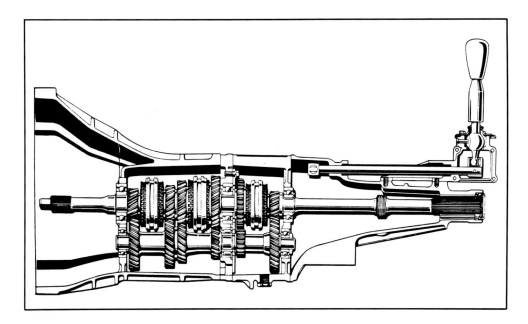

*Derived from an RX-7 gearbox, the Miata's transmission featured unique gear ratios with careful spacing and specially designed shift linkages.* **Mazda**

make it clear that you needed a close-ratio box that was closely matched to the power curve, not just close numerically; they *need* to be matched. I think some people complain that first is a little too low and second is too far from first, but in reality it goes back to the old Porsche philosophy: First is just used to get out of the pits."

Perhaps the most significant of all the driveline components came on line relatively late in the development program. This was the Power Plant Frame (PPF), an aluminum bridge that solidly connects the rear axle to the engine and transmission. Porsche and other manufacturers use similar pieces, technically called torque tubes, to tie the entire powertrain together. A car with a torque tube doesn't get jacked up and down by the torque of the driveshaft, and the time that would normally take goes straight into acceleration instead.

The PPF also ties together the front and rear of the vehicle and adds rigidity to the structure as a whole, so it helps give the Miata its wonderfully solid feel. Juddering and shaking under acceleration are virtually eliminated,

course, being located around the driveshaft, the extra weight at least went in the ideal spot: low and in the middle of the car. "It was a win/win situation," according to Garrett. "Engineering wanted it because of driveline wrap-up, the NVH [noise, vibration and harshness] guys wanted it, and the production guys said, 'If there's just four bolts, we can plug this whole thing up just like our front-wheel-drive assemblies.' The Miata, other than the number of cylinders, is

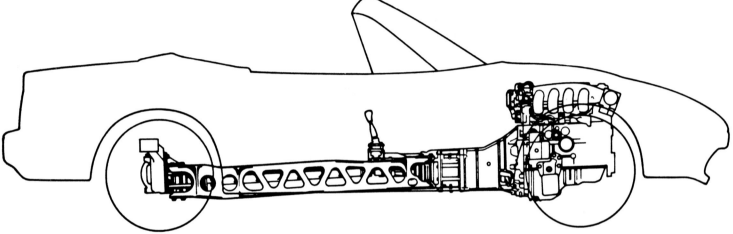

*Power Plant Frame (Mazda's name for the Miata's torque tube) united the engine and rear end, eliminating axle wind-up and considerably tightening the car's overall feel.* **Mazda**

and the car responds immediately to a shove on the gas. Strangely, though, the PPF was actually a suggestion and development of the chassis, rather than powertrain, engineers. Someone within the chassis engineering section felt their jobs would be much simpler if a torque tube were added, and one was quickly machined without the aid of blueprints just to try out the idea.

It immediately gave benefits of rigidity and throttle response, and a program was started right away on adapting one to the production car. Finite-element analysis and other computer aids were employed to determine a shape that was both light and rigid. The finished piece, a U-shaped skeletal assembly made from sheet aluminum, weighs about a dozen precious pounds, but the benefits are worth that and much more. And, of

a Ferrari Daytona in so many ways— the suspension and torque tube and everything else."

The NVH group was particularly happy to see the PPF come on line. It meant they had to isolate just four vibration points, two at the engine/transmission and two at the rear end, rather than two each at the engine, transmission and rear differential.

The front of the PPF mounts to the back of the transmission case, while the rear connects to the final-drive unit (rear differential). The final-drive unit, in turn, has a cast-aluminum housing with wide mounting arms that bolt into rubber mounts on the rear subframe of the vehicle. Equal-length halfshafts connect the rear differential to the wheels.

Finally, a viscous-controlled limited-slip differential is offered as an option. Installed, this guarantees that one rear wheel doesn't significantly overrun the other. That can be a problem if one wheel is on a slippery surface, or is lightly loaded because of hard cornering.

## Perfecting the styling

The second model to come out of MANA was—and wasn't—a big success. It was plenty clean and slick, but it somehow lacked the bold, unified statement that the team had set out to make. As an engineer, Garrett found significant value in the second model: "A lot was learned during the surface development of that second car, and a lot more was learned in the engineering package. I mean, that *was* the package compared to the first one. That really got it to where we could make something the stylists could make pretty. Much was learned from my perspective: how to get the guts in there the way we needed them. Also, compared to [the first model], you can see how much lower the cowl is; the car's starting to develop some of its low and wide stature."

From the stylist's point of view, however, model number two was important primarily as a stepping stone and, perhaps, as a direction that shouldn't be taken. "With model number two we were kind of searching around," recalls Mark Jordan. "I think we got a little too 'serious' about the shape of the car, and we left the mouth out. The car looked a lot more sophisticated, but it lost a lot of the simplistic character. I think we stood back and looked at the second model and compared it to the first, and we had to go back to that original theme

for the third and final model. But we had to go through these different stages before we could realize that we really had something in the first model."

It was the third time around that would really be the charm. At this point, of course, the competition to see who got control of the P729's styling was over: MANA had won that long ago. Now it was a matter of putting every talent at Mazda's disposal, in California *and* Japan, to work on finishing the car.

Tom Matano, Koichi Hayashi, Mark Jordan and Wu-Huang Chin were modeling away like mad in California, but Mazda's Japanese designers would also be responsible for the car's shape. MANA's designers took Chin's rounded theme for the car and began to get it together. In the sketching stages, recognizable elements of the production car's nose and tail began taking shape, and the proportions evolved to be more and more agreeable to everyone. Ultimately, however, the car would be sent to Japan for its final polish.

The Miata's Japanese and American engineering groups had no problem communicating across the Pacific. The language of engineering is precise and accurate, and a fax could illustrate the most complex concepts. Not so with the design teams. Here, it was shapes and concepts, many existing only in the designers' heads, that were being discussed. Not only that, but while engineering laws are universal, aesthetic ones are extremely regional. What looks good to a designer in America might not look good to a designer in Japan. A little confusion— and friction—was inevitable.

It was with some trepidation, then, that MANA sent their third and final full-scale model to Hiroshima. Shigenori Fukuda accompanied the model back to Japan and remained there, taking the post of general manager, Design Division. Also returning home with the clay was Shinzo Kubo, who became Hirai's right-hand man.

With the model's arrival in Japan, responsibility for the LWS's final shape fell to Shunji Tanaka, an artistically gifted designer from a respected Japanese family. To Tanaka's eye, MANA's P729 had all the makings of an exceptional design—but it wasn't quite there yet.

MANA had designed the third model with American roads and backgrounds firmly in mind. The car had an aggressive, muscular posture that evoked power in its shape. Tanaka's view was more Japanese—he wanted a more delicate, more intricate shape that took into account the Japanese respect for compactness and efficiency. To an American, the car was muscular; to a designer like Tanaka, it was overweight.

The Japanese design team set out to put the P729 on a reducing plan. One of the first steps was to shorten the wheelbase by half an inch, a move that sent Toshihiko Hirai through the roof. MANA had earlier stretched the wheelbase about a full inch, and that had been troublesome enough. Now it was happening all over again.

It wouldn't seem that a half-inch should matter to either the designer or the engineer, but both men held steadfast to their demands. The engineer pointed out that the stylist was invalidating plans that had been worked around since the beginning of the project. Tanaka insisted that the reduction was necessary to give the car the appearance it must have. Eventually the two executives came to an understanding, but Hirai was forced to relocate the battery—from behind the passenger's seat to the trunk—to work within the new wheelbase.

Tanaka then went elsewhere to lighten the look of the car. He took almost an inch and a half off the hood and deck surfaces, which could have been disastrous from an engineering standpoint. "We'd always get these

faxes from the stylists," recalls Norman Garrett, "saying, you know, 'We need the cowl to be ten more millimeters down.' And we'd just cry! There was no way at all! But finally, through some very clever engineering on Mr. Maebayashi's [the master engineer who took charge of Mazda's American engineering facilities after Shinzo Kubo] part and just some application time, we found a way to make it work."

Shunji Tanaka continued refining the shape in Japan. He

removed the black rubber rub strip that most of MANA's models had featured and left only a thin, indented character crease down the side. Details like the nose and taillamps got subtle reworking. And he worked with Wu-Huang Chin to resculpt the nose and tail ever so slightly, just enough to put a little airiness into the shapes.

In truth, all the changes Tanaka's team carried out were the sort the average person might never even notice. Most people could look at MANA's model as it was presented and

be hard pressed to know it was anything but a production Miata. But Mazda's designers are not average people—they're artists, if you will, in eye and temperament.

There were nervous staff on both sides of the Pacific when the finished model was sent back to California. MANA's designers feared for what might have happened to their child in Japan, while Tanaka and his crew feared the wrath of the Americans. It was still not too late for strong objections within the company

*The Miata combines many of the best design elements of earlier sports cars with its own unique savvy.* **Mazda**

53

to kill off the project.

Fortunately, the wrath of MANA was not to be aroused. The California crew nervously opened the crate containing Mazda's "final" MX–5 (MX–5 was becoming the most likely name for the car in production), and breathed a tremendous sigh of relief when they beheld what lay inside. The model was wonderful—and extremely true to their own concept. They cabled congratulations to Hirai, and turned out *en masse* at Los Angeles International Airport to welcome Tanaka, the hero of the day. As expected from that day on, the P729 passed its remaining tests with flying colors.

## Making it stop

Like struts, another compromise MANA was willing to accept in order to get the LWS on the road was rear drum brakes. While disc brakes are simply superior to drums, the P729 would have been light enough that lower-cost drum brakes would not have sacrificed its stopping ability too much. (A similar compromise would have been to go with a live rear axle instead of the independent unit that was finally settled upon. Mazda knew how to make a good live rear axle— they'd proven that with the first RX–7—and on the street, most drivers would never have known the difference. Happily though, that compromise was also unnecessary.)

Much to their credit, Mazda decided to give the P729 disc brakes all around despite their slightly higher cost. Four-wheel discs would virtually ensure plenty of solid, fade-free braking power for the sports car. Also, a ready donor of many of the parts could be found in an advanced package developed for the 323. Those parts consisted of 9.3 inch vented front discs and 9.1 inch solid rears. Single-piston calipers were fit all around, trailing at the front and leading at the back. To tailor the discs to the Miata, however,

*Any interior color you want, so long as it's black. Matching the airbag-equipped wheel was a main consideration for the dash design.* **Mazda**

Mazda fit a smaller power booster unit to provide more feel and improve responsiveness.

**A sports car interior**

MANA knew that they would need an interior theme for their models, as the open roadster would have looked silly without one. Traditionally, body design and interior design are two wholly separate procedures with different staffs. Since MANA consisted of few designers overall, however, the exterior designers had the rare opportunity to have something to say about the interior of their car as well.

One of the first ideas presented came from Tom Matano, who felt the dashboard of the P729 should be covered in a hard plastic that was painted body color. The effect would be that the dash was a continuation of the hoodline, the same as it had been on classics like the Austin-Healey 100 and Triumph TR-3. That idea, however, was doomed to failure because of the inability to acceptably match colors and textures between the metal hood and the plastic dash. It's doubtful that such a scheme would have made it into production anyway—reflections from the dash onto the windshield would probably have been fierce.

Wu-Huang Chin wound up having the most influence on MANA's proposed interior, and his sketches were sent on to International Automotive Design when they were chosen to build the first prototype. The V705 eventually got a futuristic wraparound interior that, while neat, really didn't fit the LWS theme. It did provide the occupants with enough comfort and convenience, however, to make the V705 enjoyable on the road.

Hiroshima decided to take over the interior design, and they started again with a clean sheet of paper. They were concerned not just with appearance but function and weight as well. Designer Kenji Matsuo kicked off the project in early 1987.

At first the team's thinking leaned toward a classic, flat panel and a three-spoke steering wheel. But the decision had already been made to supply the Miata with a driver's-side airbag, and there was no way that could be stuffed into a three-spoke wheel. The large, padded center of an airbag wheel wouldn't have looked right with a flat panel, so it was back to the drawing board.

An integral center console had always been in the plan, and Matsuo evolved it into a piece that stood out somewhat from the dash itself. Then the flat panel of some early sketches was replaced by a rounded pad, and the shape began to take hold. As time went on, drilled metal pedals began to appear, probably in an effort to add some raciness to the sketches. The idea caught on, however, and a drilled metal gas pedal made it into the production car.

The seats, originally conceived as flashy two-tone, two-piece units, matured into straightforward all-black one-piece sport seats modeled in part on Alfa Romeo chairs. Like the rest of the P729, weight was eliminated in the interior wherever possible—the Miata's seats weigh just fifty-three pounds, exceptionally little considering their high level of comfort. The door panels were also kept completely simple—some feel too simple—for the sake of reduced mass. A special frameless design was developed to keep down weight in the instrument panel.

Among the more controversial areas of the Miata interior are the folding sun visors. Project manager Hirai simply objected to solid visors on aesthetic grounds: when the top was down, one-piece visors seemed to break up the line above the windshield. To correct the problem, the visors were split in half and made foldable so they tucked up underneath the header rail (the bar across the windshield top) when not in use.

Finally, a small parcel shelf was fitted behind the seats so the Miata's occupants could stash a little extra cargo inside. In earlier sports cars, parcel shelves often gave the most storage space in the entire car. That wouldn't be possible with the MX-5, because the fuel tank had to be stuffed between the rear axle and the seats in the interest of good weight distribution. (Since the weight of fuel in the tank affects handling as it changes, good design dictated getting the tank as close to the center of the car as possible.) The parcel shelf is just large enough to allow small cases, jackets and so on to be carried in the interior but out of harm's way.

## Tops in its field

The Miata's convertible top is the new leader of the field. That credit used to go to the Alfa Romeo Spider, but the Miata's top is lighter, easier to erect and even tighter than the Italian car's.

The design of the top is an area in which Mazda gratefully acknowledges the work of International Automotive Design. IAD, coming from the land of convertible sports cars, put considerable effort into laying out the proper form for the Miata's soft top. In finished form, the Miata's one-layer top is supported by folding side links and three tubular cross-members. An indication of the thought that went into the assembly is the pair of locks that latch the top to the header rail. Usually, these are simple cast hooks or clips. On the Miata, however, they're well-finished fasteners with secondary locking buttons for added safety. The locks even feature specially designed pivot points to add leverage during locking, making for a secure fit and a tight roof.

*Until a very late date, the seven-spoke sport wheel came to America with a dished and polished center spinner.* **John Lamm**

# CHAPTER THREE

# Miata Maintenance

Taking care of sports cars used to be an art. Their care and feeding was a lengthy, arcane ritual with myriad rules that had to be remembered to keep the Leaky God appeased. Keeping an MG or Alfa Romeo on the road was only slightly less complicated than child rearing, and it quickly separated the sports car fans from the poseurs.

Fortunately, the Miata won't put its owners through anything like the tribulations of those earlier sports cars. There are no special gizmos to oil, no leaky carburetors to tune and rebuild every weekend, and no gymnastic convolutions needed to get the top up and down. That's not to say that your shiny new roadster won't appreciate some tender loving care. Sports cars have personalities, and the Miata's, like any other car's, will turn sour if you abuse it.

Americans are unique when it comes to car care—they don't do it. The average American grew up with big, low-revving engines that held together despite considerable neglect. That "luxury" has let most of us get out of good maintenance habits. The average Pontiac V–8 would run forever two quarts low on oil, something that

could never be said of a European sports car. Europeans and Japanese, on the other hand, grew up with tight, small engines that simply forced them to keep a close eye on the vital fluids. Lightweight materials like aluminum made for closer observation still.

## Oil

Oil is the most important fluid in any engine. While the engine's running, a fine film of oil separates rotating parts like the crankshaft from the bearings they ride in. In other words, pieces that seem to be touching actually aren't making contact at all. That's the secret to how an engine can withstand the brutal demands asked of it.

Once you know why an engine needs oil, you can see how critical it is that plenty of clean oil is available at all times. A lack of oil allows metal-to-metal contact, and dirty lubricant carries grit that gouges the parts it's trying to protect. As oil ages, it loses its ability to film over parts—which is why it needs to be changed instead of just topped up.

Finally, as the oil level in the engine falls off from leaking or

window while the roof is folded, lay a soft, clean towel over it before dropping the rest of the roof into the well.

**Keeping water out of the car**

Water and cars don't mix. There's nothing that can be done about that combination when it happens on the outside, and manufacturers go to great lengths to prevent corrosion and

*Right after a sudden southern California downpour is about the only time you'll see a West Coast Miata with its top up.* **Mazda**

cracking from taking place. With metal and plastic pieces, it's a problem that can be licked.

With soft pieces like seats and carpets, though, the factory can only do so much. Mazda waterseals and weatherproofs the soft pieces of the Miata as best they can, but the interior's longevity is predicated on keeping most of the water outside where it belongs.

The most common water entry points on the Miata are around the glass perimeters. A thrilling weekend activity to British car owners of days gone by was adjusting the windows to fit the top, an ordeal that always left

them wondering how people from such a rainy country could be so inept at weathersealing their cars. The trouble was that the top inevitably shrank, shifted and flexed over time, and soon the windows didn't meet correctly with the roof anymore. Moisture then entered the cabin and soon there was an unpleasant pool of mildewed water, cigarette butts and old French fries in the passenger's footwell. A stray spark from the crummy Lucas electrics under the dashboard could easily spawn a new life form in this soup.

Eventually, the Miata will have the same leakage problem, though it will take quite a bit longer. (Well, maybe it won't *ever* get to the primordial soup stage, but the windows *will* need to be adjusted.) The first indication that something is wrong is usually wind noise, not water leaks, and this is the time to take care of the problem. To adjust the windows you first need to get the door panels off, and that's tricky if you've never done it before. If you have a service manual and the proper tools, by all means do the job yourself; otherwise, take the car to a dealer and pay for the service. The money you save in water damage to the interior will more than pay for the repair itself.

Wind noise and leaks can also be caused by some fault in the weatherstripping around the windows and header rail. Especially sensitive is the area above the side windows where the rubber is split so the roof can fold. Periodically check the rubber weatherstripping—it should be smooth, flexible, complete and free of cracks. If some flaw is found, the whole strip should be replaced. Here again, the money for the repair should be seen as an investment: pay a little now or a lot later. You should also get in the habit of periodically checking the roof for small tears or cracks, particularly at the rear where it joins the bodywork.

Finally, if you notice moist patches or standing water anywhere in the car—the footwells, under or behind the seats and especially in the trunk—it's imperative to trace and correct the cause immediately. Again, an occasional accident is no big deal; repeated exposure could cause serious damage, however.

Sometimes nothing can be done about a little moisture getting in the car. Everybody who's ever owned a convertible has left the top down on a gorgeous day, gone into a restaurant for lunch and come out to a sudden squall and a car full of rain. Once the damage is done, get the water up as quickly as possible, with towels or whatever's handy, and then dry out the interior with the floor heater. An occasional washing won't ruin the interior; it's standing water or repeated soakings that need to be strenuously avoided.

## Security

One distinct disadvantage of the soft top is its susceptibility to nasty little parking-lot denizens. Whether to gain entry into the car or simply to ruin your day, there are people out there who'd love nothing better than to slice through your snug vinyl roof.

The best way to protect yourself is to watch where you park. The same rules that apply to all cars go double for convertibles like the Miata. Use a garage whenever you can, or try to get as much light—from street lights, shop windows or what have you—onto the car if one's not available. And try to park in high-traffic areas near the fronts of stores and theaters, on busy streets and so forth.

Easily removed items like leather jackets and cameras should be locked in the trunk, never the passenger compartment. If something must be left in the cockpit, at least try to hide it out of sight in one of the locking bins or behind the seats. Remember that getting into a locked convertible is as easy as a pass of a switchblade. Nothing is absolutely safe inside the car when you're not around.

Some people leave their convertibles intentionally unlocked, thinking it's better to let thieves get in through the door and do less damage, rather than going through the top and getting the goods anyway. This is a depressing outlook, particularly since many insurance policies won't pay off for items removed from an unlocked car, but not an uncommon one.

The optional hardtop eliminates all these problems, though it creates a few of its own. First of all, where do you put it when you're not using it? It weighs nearly forty-five pounds, and its size makes it tough to lift on and off alone.

One answer is a hardtop hoist, an old favorite of Corvette and Jaguar E-Type owners. A hoist is just a pulley system set up in your own garage and located so the hardtop can be lifted on and off by one person. Setting up a hoist can be lots of trouble, though, so most people just handle the top the old-fashioned way or ask a friend to help.

Another potential problem with the hardtop is having it rub against the

*A heavy coat of wax on the deck should prevent the hardtop's weatherstripping from scuffing the paint.* **Mazda**

Next page

*Optional hardtop quickly transforms the Miata from convertible sports car to snug GT. But where do you put the SMC (sheet-molding compound) roof when it's not in use?* **Mazda**

body, eventually wearing through the paint. Keeping an extra-heavy coat of wax on the area where the deck meets the top is your best protection.

## Things to carry at all times

Some things should be carried in every car: a simple first-aid kit, basic tools, extra fuses and so on. Triple-A can give you a better list than this book can, so let's concentrate on extras that are handy to have specifically in a car like the Miata. All of these things will fit into one small box, or they can be shoved unceremoniously into the otherwise wasted nooks and crannies of the Miata's trunk.

### Gloves

On a clear but cool day, the things most likely to get cold are your hands. It's a shame to have to put the top up just to keep your fingers warm, so keep an old pair of wool or insulated leather gloves handy. Stay away from mittens, which make it tough to work the interior controls.

### Old sweater or jacket

Like gloves, an old sweater can keep you from having to put the top up on a less-than-balmy day. Even a heavy jacket will fit up above the collapsible spare, which is an oddly shaped area that's almost never used otherwise. Any sweater or jacket you consign to the trunk is going to have to spend its whole life there—it will get plenty dirty, plenty fast.

### Hat with a brim

The sun's always getting in your eyes in a convertible, and a decent cap with a brim goes a long way toward alleviating the annoying and possibly dangerous problem. It's a good idea to go with an adjustable one that can be tightened down on the highway, then loosened up around town so your brain gets some blood occasionally.

### Duct tape

Just the thing to temporarily patch a roof that's been accidentally or deliberately cut. It pays to buy the expensive kind; the cheap stuff will

leave lots of ugly glue behind. Black duct tape will of course be less unsightly than the silver variety, but any tape at all looks shoddy. If you're 300 miles from home in a thunderstorm, though, looks don't matter much one way or another—staying dry does.

### Terrycloth towels

For when water manages to make it into the car.

70

**Trash bag**
    To keep stray papers from flying out of the car when you're driving with the top down.

**Personal goodies**
    Lip balm. Sunscreen. Throat lozenges. A handkerchief. Sunglasses. Think of anything you like to have with you outdoors, then ask yourself if a constant 65 mph wind blast would make you want it even more.

*Top down and snow on the ground—warm clothing can let you enjoy your convertible year-round.* **Peter Vance Studios**

### Small flashlight

One thing the MX–5 lacks is a decent map light. The underdash interior lighting is marginal at best for reading small things; for navigating with a large map it's hopeless.

It's possible to rig up all sorts of aftermarket interior lights, but the best solution is simply to go out and buy a small, tough flashlight. Both Mag-Lite and Coleman make excellent miniature aluminum flashlights that fit in the glovebox or console.

*Up and off: Interior control holds the headlights up for washing. Dirty lights seriously diminish night vision.* **Mazda**

### Keeping the car clean and preventing rust

One of the easiest and most important elements of maintaining any car is keeping it clean. Clean cars don't rust nearly as quickly as dirty ones, and their paint stays brighter longer. It's also easier to detect and repair paint scratches and chips if you wash the car often, and a clean car is likely to get better service from your mechanic.

On warm afternoons, washing the car can actually be fun. In cold climates, though, there's sometimes no choice but to run it through an automatic car wash. This definitely gets the dirt off the paint, but automatic car washes often do considerable damage by stripping off the wax and leaving tiny scratches, to say nothing of trashing the soft plastic rear window. On the road, a self-serve wand-type car wash is a much better alternative. If you do go through an automatic wash, though, at least remember to unscrew the antenna from the back of the car. It's usually just finger tight, but if you can't take it out by hand, use a small wrench. If you don't take it off yourself, the machines in the car wash will probably do it for you.

If at all possible, it's better to wash the car yourself. That means getting the right tools: a bucket, a hose, a large car-washing sponge and a chamois or some soft, clean, fluffy towels. Try not to use any soap, which strips away wax and other protectants from the car's finish, leaving the bare paint exposed to the elements. If the car's simply too dirty for water alone, find an automotive soap that's formulated not to remove wax. They can be had at almost any auto parts store.

The trick to a good wash is lots of water and a shady place. Douse the entire car and wipe off the dirt with a dripping sponge while the metal's still good and wet. Keep rinsing the sponge in fresh water and wetting down the car through the whole procedure. The idea is to float the dirt away—if you let the sponge or the metal dry out you'll wind up scraping dirt particles along the surface of the car itself. That leads to tiny scratches that quickly ruin the finish. Sunshine speeds up the drying process and leaves mineral deposits from the water, so find a cool, shady spot if you can. Never wash a car in full sun.

When the entire car has been

hours an MG would have taken quite a bit more out of us.

Another hour of Interstate and I couldn't take it anymore. Not the cockpit, which was fine, but the long, straight expanse of freeway. I heeled the nose off at the next exit ramp and we headed into the woods.

How wise was it to set off into snow country without chains or snow tires? Not very, certainly. Fortunately, the gods smiled down on us, and any trouble we might have gotten into the Miata's optional limited-slip diff got us out of again. The viscous-controlled differential gave amazingly smooth and progressive operation. Only once did it take any more than judicious use of the throttle to get the car going. (In a parking lot both rear wheels wound up on ice, and it took some fancy crabbing to extricate the car. It would have been easy to push it out, but who wants to mess up a new pair of boots?)

I can only imagine how well the diff would work on the tight, fast corners of a racetrack, because on the slick corners of backroad New England it worked wonders. Between the overall stability of the Miata's platform, the good grip of the tires and the limited-slip rear diff, my initial wariness of slipping the tail out on ice and snow quickly gave way to almost complete confidence. Too complete, in fact, as I was reminded a few times by the inevitable sharp drift to the outside of a turn, the car moving from dry pavement to ice.

If the car felt balanced on slick surfaces, it was absolutely solid on dry ones. The Miata had all the right hardware: superb weight distribution, good tires, a rigid body and carefully designed suspension bits. It lived up to and beyond its promise.

One of the things that amazed me when I first started getting reports of this car was that many of the testers felt it was the easiest car to drive fast that they'd ever sampled. This was no batch of neophytes, either—these were people who'd done their time in

Ferraris, Porsches and Corvettes, not just inexpensive Japanese machinery. If this crowd was impressed by the car, I knew I was in for a treat when I got *my* chance behind the wheel.

But OK, enough of the party line for a moment. The road trip did point up a few things that annoyed me about the Miata, and I might as well put them down here as anywhere. First of all, folding sun visors may seem like a good idea but I don't like them. They don't have enough rigidity to let the driver manhandle the visor from side to side, which he or she must do during fast driving into the sun. It takes a careful touch to position the visor, and that takes longer than it should.

The visors' mounting points also bothered me. Because they're mounted far up under the header rail, they can't be pushed up into little spoilers sticking above the windshield line. Any MG veteran will tell you that this is the only way to tailor the top-down wind bubble exactly to your liking.

I also found the blind spots of the soft top annoying, although I readily admit that this car should be driven top-down anyway. Sometimes a closed canopy is mandatory, though, and in those cases the roof often seemed to be exactly in the places I wanted to look out. When merging into traffic you have to remember the blind spots and crane your noggin accordingly.

Finally, those eyeball vents on the dash have got to go. It's not that they're a bad idea; it's just that they're too hard to adjust quickly and accurately. Maybe Mazda should put some kind of knob in the middle so drivers can get a better grip on them. Maybe they should make the sockets larger. Whatever it takes, something must be done.

Otherwise, the controls and details of the car impressed me as excellent. The shoulder harnesses, for instance, were easier to use in the Miata than in any other convertible I've driven. The gauges and controls have all been laid out in perfectly logical, easy-to-reach locations, including the climate controls and radio.

As for the rest of the road trip, the Miata was a companion that, unlike the great sports cars of the past, was not also a part-time adversary. I calculated a rough mpg reading in the mid-twenties for the weekend, particularly impressive since so much of the backroad driving was done out of fifth gear. Mechanical problems were nonexistent. Untoward behavior, at least on the car's part, was nonexistent as well.

on the subject: "If you want to go fast, shift at seven grand or 6500, and let the engine develop those 120 horses that it will at 6500. It's like a door hinge—it's meant to be swung open."

This was just brought home to me while driving a friend's Honda CRX. I let the engine wind up to a natural 5500 rpm while passing a truck, and he suddenly got very quiet. Finally, he asked why was I abusing his car like that—and, incidentally, how was I getting it to go so *fast*?

## Driving the Miata

If the Miata is your first real sports car, you might be thinking you'll have to forget everything you think you know about driving. Well, you can remember to check your blind spot and let pedestrians have the right of way, but there are definitely some things that require special handling in a sports car.

Let's take shift points first, an area where many new sports car owners have trouble. (A shift point is just that: the point at which you shift gears up or down.) The first thing to remember with the Miata is to *wind it out*. American drivers are so used to torquey, low-revving engines that it's virtually impossible to get most of them to rev a small-displacement four as much as they should. Norman Garrett has already laid out his feelings

*Logical, clean dashboard and controls make the driver quickly at home—something that could never be said of yesterday's sports cars.*
**Mazda**

The sound of a fast-revving engine is associated with imminent destruction by many Yanks, and it's a tough habit to break. An engine makes its maximum torque—which governs acceleration—only at a given rpm, and with the Miata that point is higher on the tachometer than you might think: 5500 rpm.

Of course, you can rev the engine *too* hard. How fast will the thing turn before it starts throwing chunks through the hood? On the Miata, there's a fuel cutoff that keeps the engine from running that quickly at all. But the faster the engine is turning the more stress on the pistons, wristpins,

valves and so on, so if you're just tooling around town you can go a little easier. High shift points might be noisier than necessary and won't get you through traffic any more quickly. In these cases, keeping the engine between 2250 and 4500 rpm might provide you with plenty of around-town performance.

To keep the engine in the proper rev range it's important to be able to make smooth shifts. Shifting up is easy, or at least easier than shifting down. The trick to both is the same: matching engine speed to wheel speed before letting out the clutch.

On upshifts, this becomes second nature. You come out of first, put the stick into second, start letting out the clutch and give the engine enough gas to make the transition smooth. It's simple.

Downshifting, though—say going from second to first—is tougher. The engine has to be sped up much more during a downshift than an upshift, and missing the mark causes more of a lurch. So the drill is: clutch in, change down a gear (or however many gears you think are right), blip the engine up to speed, then clutch out. Sounds simpler than it is, though it's a maneuver that practice rewards greatly.

Double-clutching, a once mandatory downshifting skill, is not strictly necessary with the Miata, but entertaining nonetheless. Double-clutching adds one more step to the downshift—the clutch is let out quickly while the gearshift is in between gears. In other words: clutch in, shift to neutral, clutch out; then clutch in again, shift into the proper gear and clutch out once more. Double-clutching used to be necessary in the days before synchromesh; today it's more a matter of fun, though it does put less strain on the gearbox than a straight shift.

One step up is the heel-and-toe downshift, sometimes necessary because drivers are a bit shy in the leg

department when it comes to braking and changing down at the same time. You need your left foot for the clutch, your right foot for the brake and another right foot to blip the engine up to speed.

The solution is to use your right

foot to brake and squeeze the throttle at the same time. The toes stay on the brake while you get on the gas with your heel. Again, practice makes perfect on this one.

It's also critical to learn where the corners of the car are. Head out to an empty parking lot with some traffic cones—plumber's friends or even paper cups will work if you don't have any pylons—and get an idea of how close you can come without hitting them. When you know where the ends of the car are you can start to place it where

*Knowing where your car's corners are lets you place it exactly where you want it on the road.* **Mazda**

you want on the road.

Another skill the Miata rewards greatly is smoothness. Try to make all transitions—left to right, brake to gas, corner to straight—as smooth and gentle as possible. You'll go faster and have more control in the bargain.

## Future classics versus current classics

Perhaps it's not fair to compare a new, low-cost, mass-produced car with the recognized sports car classics of days gone by. Not fair to the recognized classics, that is.

The MX–5 Miata should simply be a better car than any of them. There isn't a single objective area in which it should not outperform the likes of MGs, Alfas, Fiats or Triumphs. But that's a claim many cars can honestly make, a simple fact of modern technology. The Austin-Healey 100–4 was designed forty years ago by a few insightful men using pencils and paper; the Miata was constructed by hundreds of skilled, high-tech designers and engineers with the assistance of super-mainframe computers and four decades of advanced chassis and engine technology. Of course, then again you never know . . . a 1962 Jaguar E-Type will still mop up the road with ninety-five percent of the 1990 cars out there.

Perhaps it's more enlightening to look at what is *not* quantifiable: the subjective feel of the Miata versus that of some earlier cars. The feel of the Miata was consciously and painstakingly engineered, but there was considerable doubt in some corners that such a process could lead to what enthusiasts were looking for. Some people said it was like trying to get 100 composers to write a single symphony.

### Miata versus Alfa Romeo

The first thing you notice about the Alfa Spider, a mint-condition 1971 in this case, is the apparently odd layout of the controls. The gearshift sprouts from halfway between the floor and the dash and the throttle pedal perches strangely to one side. The adjustable seat reclines comfortably, but the pedals all seem too close and the steering wheel seems too far away—typically Italian. You quickly get the hang of the Alfa interior, but even then it's not as comfortable or agreeable as the Miata's.

The clutch takes up nicely in good European fashion—as nicely as the Mazda's—but the gear changes seem yards long compared to the Miata's quick throws. The long stick doesn't help matters, nor does the slightly vague feeling between gates. All told, the Alfa gearbox is predictable; it feels like you should wire ahead to the next gear for a reservation.

The Alfa definitely lacks the power, both low- and high-end, of the

*The Alfa Spider's beautiful Pininfarina body hides lots of nice things: twin-cam engine, decent quality, great sounds, a leather interior and spirited—if aging—handling.*
**Lamm-Morada Publishing**

88

Mazda—or is that a factor of the whippy driveline? Step on the gas and there's plenty of noise but not much acceleration. If ever there was a good argument for Miata-style torque tubes, it's this car.

The sound itself, however, is nicer than the MX–5's bass exhaust note, which no doubt gives the perfectionist Mazda engineers conniptions. Where the Japanese car blasts out a single solid note, the Alfa has a wonderful two-tone sound. Ironically, it's doubtful that Alfa Romeo spent much time tuning the exhaust of the Spider, while Mazda put all sorts of grief into getting just the right noise out the tailpipe.

The top on the Alfa was known as the best in the business until the Miata came along. The Alfa's brakes are solid and rewarding, but no match for the modern car's all-disc binders. Nor is the handling, for the Spider simply dates back to a time when standards were different. Tires weren't too good when the Alfa was penned, so extremely rigid structures wouldn't have been much benefit even if the technology had been around to build them.

Today, though, it's literally unsettling to experience such a willowy car. There's a noticeable amount of flex in the corners and cowl shake over bumps, and it never feels like the front and rear ends are really working together. Where the Mazda works as an entire piece, you have to keep giving attention to individual bits of the Alfa. To some people that's the car's charm; to others, merely an aggravation. The Spider's suspension was nice when new and is a little outdated now, but it's still rewarding. The ride is about as supple as the Mazda's, but there's considerable body roll in corners and a bit of wander over bumps.

The Alfa's rear end is extremely easy to hang out in long, gentle powerslides, a factor of its low overall grip. It's great fun, at least until you perform the same maneuver in the Miata and see how much more precise

and controllable the action is and at how much faster a speed it can be performed.

The Alfa's a bigger car than the Mazda, and feels it. There's a lot more inertia getting the Spider around corners, and the much higher lean angles accentuate that feeling. There's actually more room in the Alfa's cabin, but from the driver's seat it feels more cramped. The Miata's excellent shoulder room is the key here.

Subjectively, both cars feel great in their own way. The Alfa's a blast because of the willing, enjoyable way it takes to corners and straights—even if it can't take care of either particularly fast. And with that classic Pininfarina body, the top down and the twin exhausts singing their favorite aria at 65 mph, all's right with the world in the Alfa Spider. But getting back to the original question: Does the Alfa have a certain soul that's lacking in the Miata? Perhaps. To some people, it's the same difference that separates Kevin Costner from Sean Connery—there's simply nothing that can be done about one's youth.

**Miata versus MGB**

The best way to find a like-new MGB is to find a *new* MGB. British Motor Heritage of England is indeed building new MGBs or more precisely, building completely new MGB bodyshells from the original jigs and tools. BMH then sells the shells to be refitted with the running gear from an existing, presumably rusty MG. If that running gear has been decently rebuilt, the result is virtually a new car.

That seemed just the thing to go up against the Miata. What I found was a 1969 spec MGB built from a Heritage platform. At a cost of more than $10,000 all told, this is not a cheap car. It's still less expensive than a Miata, though, and should hold its value better for the next ten years. On the other hand, like-new or not, the MGB still sported SU carburetors and Lucas electronics—a sure-fire recipe for roadside repairs.

The MGB has been a perennial favorite sports car since 1962: Everybody had one, everybody alternately loved and hated it and once the beast was gone from their garages everyone missed it immensely. What made the car so successful?

For one thing, almost half a million MGBs were cranked out over the course of eighteen years, so there were always plenty of cheap used ones around for young enthusiasts. For another, it was truly an endearing, if not very advanced, automobile. Aside from the exasperating (but easily repaired) intake and electrical systems,

*MG figured that this 1976 MGB was its one-millionth automobile. But their celebration was tempered by the raised height, heavy and ugly bumpers, and power-sapping intake system that federal regulations had forced onto the car.* **Lamm-Morada Publishing**

the MGB was a tough little car. And it loved to run, urging (or was that luring?) the driver on ever longer and longer trips. This car had lots of personality, and most of it was good.

Even by today's standards the MGB is quite a solid car. It's much more rigid than the competition from Alfa, Fiat and Triumph, and the

handling is precise up to a point; once the live rear axle starts coming around, that's your cue to back off.

A lot of the MGB's rigidity came from simply using plenty of steel. It's heavy for its size while not being particularly crashworthy, and its decent handling comes at the expense of suspension travel and a smooth ride. While the front end tracks extremely well, the rear hops around during hard cornering on all but the smoothest surfaces. With lots of power, wide tires and a smooth track, the MGB might feel like the Miata. In the real world, though, the difference is like night and day.

The Miata hustles into bumpy corners and tracks through them with glee. The MG makes you feel that every pothole could be your last. All in all, the MGB gives a good performance but not one in the Miata's league. At one time the MGB was as sophisticated a car as most people could expect or even imagine, but today it seems positively archaic. To many, that in itself may be a recommendation.

The MGB is, however, a car with loads of personality. It strikes up an immediate rapport with the driver. A slightly more "masculine" car than its competition, the steering, brakes and clutch require a fair amount of muscle, and the exhaust note is low and throaty. Trying to shift quickly is a great substitute for Nautilus equipment; taking your time, however, makes the gearbox a delight.

Finally, the pushrod engine is unsportingly reluctant to rev. It has plenty of grunt at low rpm but runs out of steam as it approaches a rather nerve-wracking redline of 6000 rpm. The MGB feels faster than the Miata right off the line, but soon the torquey engine runs out of steam. By the time you're shifting the MGB into second the Miata is just coming on the power in first, and from there it's no contest. The Miata is significantly faster in both straight-line acceleration and cornering speed. Like the Miata, though, the MG is remarkably solid and thoroughly enjoyable. If the English could build a car today that's as excellent for its time as the MGB was for 1962, they might give Mazda some reason to look over their shoulder.

## Miata versus Spitfire

In 1962, Standard-Triumph introduced the diminutive Spitfire as a competitor to the Austin-Healey Sprite. The Spit was a nice enough shape (one of the few Michelotti designs that could make that claim) and a spirited performer—slow but seeming faster than it was.

Updates kept the car modern, which was fine when that simply meant enlarging the engine every few years. When modern times mandated big bumpers and emissions strangulation, however, it would probably have been better to let the little car die a dignified death.

The Spitfire was a likable, refreshingly small and some would say unremarkable sports car. Why unremarkable? It simply never got taken seriously, much like the Austin-Healey Sprite/MG Midget it took on in the marketplace. In America, at least, the Spitfire was a tiny car in a land of giants; it was often perceived almost as a toy, even by diehard enthusiasts who should have known better.

The Spitfire played an important role in the birth of the Miata, however. Both MANA and Hiroshima had resident Spits, and impromptu drives in these expatriate Triumphs went a long way toward stirring up enthusiasm in some recalcitrant souls. Let loose in an honest-to-goodness sports car for the first time in Lord knows how long, more than one dubious executive came back with a big smile on his face and a new belief in Mazda's proposed LWS.

Norman Garrett, a confirmed Spitfire fan, remembers the saga of MANA's own white Triumph: "In the engineering department we were looking for concept cars, and we bought that white one. It was a neat car and gorgeous when we bought it, but it was a lesson in what not to build. The doors didn't latch. The top didn't work. It overheated. We took it on test trips, and the poor Spitfire . . . it was just the sickest little thing."

Garrett had an affection for the car, though, and he tried to buy it when he left MANA in 1987: "But they said 'We need it for one more thing.' And I said 'What, a crash test?'"

Aside from its fragility, the baby Triumph was a good comparison model for many of the styling and testing sessions the Miata went through. Roughly the same size as the Miata, though, somehow the Spitfire always seemed a bit insubstantial. The Miata proves that the Spitfire's shape and construction, not its size, were responsible.

Smaller than cars like the MGB and Alfa Romeo, the Spitfire was also slower. But with its light weight and independent rear axle—a primitive but enjoyable example—it promised to be a fun car to drive. The Triumph's main drawback was always its truly fragile construction, but that wasn't likely to bother me on one afternoon drive. Dan

*Smaller than most sports cars—about the Miata's size—the Triumph Spitfire brought independent rear suspension and low overall weight to the masses.* **Lamm-Morada Publishing**

Fitch's 1972 Spitfire was fresh out of a full restoration and promised to be a thrill.

Compared to the Miata, the Spitfire fell down badly. Its charm against cars like the MGB was always its small size; with the Miata taking that distinction away from it, the Spitfire found itself without a strong card to play. Its sound was less distinctive than many other classics, its performance a bit shy and its interior

*One of the few ways to make a Miata look big is to put it in front of two Lotus Elan race cars.* **Michael C. Sharp**

layout bordered on the perverse. For the money, however—pretty decent Spits can still be had for $1,000 or less—the baby Triumph offers the same superlight thrills as the Miata for a mere fraction of the cost. While the Miata feels light and solid, though, the Spitfire felt like . . . well . . . a *toy*.

**Miata versus Lotus Elan**

Now we come to the serious competition. Forget that the Lotus Elan is a fragile, tiny car made literally of plastic. Forget that it's so small it makes the Miata look positively porcine. And forget that the Elan driver has about as much interior room as John Glenn did in *Friendship 7*. The Elan deserves respect—a lot of respect—for being perhaps the ultimate example of the Lightweight Sports Car concept.

Lotus was a race car constructor with a kit-car sideline at the time the Elan came around, and their record over the road was less than admirable. Their record on the track, however, was superlative. In the decade gone by before the Elan, Lotus cars won everything up to and including the Formula One Constructor's Championship.

Many of the company's earlier offerings were streetable machines after a fashion, but only one—the fiberglass Elite—made any pretense of being a real road car. The Elite was a magnificently designed, superlatively fast, horribly built little disaster of a car. It was terribly fragile and poorly assembled at the factory, to say nothing of the job the final customer might do in installing the running gear—for the Elite was still offered as a kit. Though brilliantly designed, it did little to enhance Lotus' financial coffers or its general image.

The company's next street effort was the Elan, and this car was relatively more successful. Rather than the Elite's all-fiberglass construction, the Elan used a fiberglass body supported by a steel backbone frame. The engine, final drive and suspension hung off the frame, rather than the body as they had on the Elite, and the Elan was a roadster while the Elite had been a coupe.

It was, however, still a Lotus, which meant that reliability and toughness had been sacrificed early on to achieve the car's stunning low weight: less than 1,300 pounds in its most basic form. Furthermore, to keep aerodynamic drag down, the car was made as compact, short and narrow as possible.

The Elan ran—oh, how it ran— but not necessarily for long. No matter what the build quality was like, though, it was a uniquely appealing automobile. It was tiny and light, and the engines that went into it were all high-winding and powerful. Eventually came the big-valve Sprint engine with

126 bhp, which was the engine in my test car.

If you know how a 2,200 pound Miata feels with 116 horses, imagine a 1,300 pound Elan with 126. The Elan was conceived as being the closest a buyer could get to a street-legal racing car, and it hit the mark perhaps too well. Let out the light clutch, and the engine takes up immediately. The rear end will slew to the side if you're not careful with the throttle, and the Elan leaps ahead with ease. One block and you can tell this fragile rocket will take the Miata in a fair fight: chase it down, chew it up and spit it out a half mile down the road. Assuming, that is, that it holds together.

Behind the wheel the Elan immediately makes its size known. The interior doesn't feel cramped, but that's only because the driver's having too much fun: heaven help the passenger. From inside, the Elan also seems a bit elderly. It creaks and flexes, rattles and bangs. The gauges betray the overall fragility of the car itself, their needles jumping wildly over bumps and the wires falling down from under the dash. The Elan lacks the solid feel of the Miata, though the steering, brakes and accelerator are all wonderfully responsive. As much as the Miata feels all one piece, the Elan lets you know it's a collection of pieces.

And yet the components work beautifully in concert. The Lotus and the Miata share a rare ability to make the driver feel attached to the road. In the Mazda, it's a benefit of solidity; in the Lotus, one of light weight and passionate engineering.

The Miata's not as fast as the Elan, a factor of the Lotus' superior power-to-weight ratio. But the Miata is a real car, while the Elan is something you'd only own as a third or fourth vehicle. What the Lotus has is spirit, and a design that moves the driver to great heights under the right conditions. From the dispassionate viewpoint of a non-owner, the Elan is the more interesting car. You feel that there's much to learn from the car, lots of mystery in its mechanicals. For an owner, of course, that feeling might simply translate into nervous terror.

The Elan also has one of the nicest shapes in sports car history, and the Miata's body is quite reminiscent of it. "The Elan captures the essence of what we wanted to capture as far as the philosophy goes," remarks MANA designer Mark Jordan. "A very simple, elegant kind of timeless design. The Elan lacks some of the personality that we put into the Miata . . . the Miata's got more animation about it. But basically [both cars are] a simple, straightforward shape that's pretty long lasting."

From the driver's seat, the similarities shouldn't be surprising. The Elan, as the premier LWS of recent memory, was in some ways a target of Mazda's engineers as well. "One that stands out in particular," recalls Norman Garrett, "was on a test trip we took in Japan. We had a Lotus Seven, a Lotus Elan, a Reliant Scimitar from England, an X1/9, a Porsche 911 Cabriolet, and an MGB. We went up into the mountains, and the amazing thing to me was the Elan: The shocks were bad on it and it had a lot of body roll, but it was the fastest car up and down the mountain. And it was also the most confidence-inspiring car up and down that mountain."

That Elan became something of a catalyst in getting the Miata's development team to work with one mind. "It just had the neatest feeling to me," Garrett continues, "and that was the personality of one man, Colin Chapman, coming through in nuts and bolts." Back at Hiroshima, Garrett tried to put that feeling into words. "'We've got to think like one guy,'" he told his fellow engineers. "'We've got to get that fire in our soul like we had when we were doing that four-wheel drift down the mountain tonight.' My speech didn't do it, but somehow everybody grew to that goal, and everybody did start to think like one man."

In more objective terms, their attempt was to capture the wonderfully light, communicative feel of the Elan without sacrificing usability or strength. What they have created is a car that does just that. Given your ultimate Miata driver, forget it. There are much better driving books out there written by much better drivers.

If you're serious about extracting the most from your Miata, though, rather than just settling for a book, you might want to look into an advanced driving school like the ones

*Duane Simpson pits during an Escort Endurance race with the Simpson Brothers Racing/Miata Club of America competition car.* **Miata Club of America**

choice of either car for five hot laps around a racetrack, you'd still go for the Elan. Given the choice of taking either one home from the pits, the Miata wins hands down.

### Driving school and racing

If you're reading this book hoping to learn how to become the run by Bob Bondurant, Skip Barber or Bertil Roos. The Miata Club of America is also organizing a series of driving schools to be taught by Sports Car Club of America racer Duane Simpson. These schools will teach you in hands-on track sessions the finer points of car control, not just toward a racing career but for actual, everyday use. They'll make you a safer, faster, smoother and smarter driver, and teach you all about the things you've been doing wrong behind the wheel these many years. What these schools will teach doesn't come cheap. But if it saves you from being in an accident, and it might, it'll pay for itself many times over. Furthermore, it will show you how to at least come close to extracting the maximum fun and enjoyment out of your new Miata.

As long as you're going to school anyway, why not try a little racing to boot? The Miata is so new that no one's really sure where it will fit in the racing scene of the 1990s. Even Duane Simpson—who, as half of Simpson Brothers Racing, is the Miata Club of America's competition director—is uncertain.

No one would be happier than Simpson to see the Miata made eligible for the same SCCA Production classes that consist mostly of modified MGs, Fiats, Alfas and Triumphs. "If it ran against a production car now with production rules, I have a feeling it would beat every single one," he asserts. "Most of them are running maybe 100 horsepower, and with [the Miata], if you put on a completely open exhaust, tuned like you can, and did the suspension as they can, there really wouldn't be any competition." For that very reason, he doubts the car will ever be made eligible for those classes.

Simpson knows of what he speaks because, in conjunction with the Miata Club of America, Simpson Brothers Racing fielded the first serious Miata racing effort in the country. The entry came in SCCA Escort Endurance, a series for essentially stock sports cars, and the virtually unmodified Escort car ran almost the same lap times as highly modified Production racers.

The MCA Miata was so close to stock that only aftermarket wheels, a rollcage, an onboard fire system and a raceworthy driver's seat gave away its competition intentions. Simpson

Brothers Racing didn't even bother to balance and blueprint the car (tear down the engine and machine its internal parts to perfect true). "If we did that, the most we figured we could gain is maybe five horsepower, and I doubt if we could even get that—the Japanese are pretty good when they build their motors. I didn't see spending $6,000 to gain five horsepower when we could get it other ways just in tuning," Simpson says.

Whether the MCA/Simpson Brothers Miata would continue in Showroom Stock, as it's called, depended on the flurry of rule changes that were being introduced for the 1990 season. Before the season opened, it looked like large Escort Endurance racers, including the Chevrolet Camaro and Mazda RX-7, would be forced to run in strictly stock form while smaller cars like the Miata and Honda CRX would be allowed a fair degree of modifications. Until the final

formula was settled upon, however, Simpson Brothers Racing had no way to gauge their chances for the coming season.

The same trouble with rule changes affected International Motor Sports Association's own Showroom Stock class, the Firestone Firehawk. Rod Millen had laid the groundwork

*Though the hardtop adds precious pounds, its benefits in safety and aerodynamics are a fair trade in racing.* **Miata Club of America**

for a Miata effort there, but IMSA was still not sure whether it would OK the MX-5 for competition. If it did, the Miata's light weight, good handling and excellent fuel mileage might well make it a winner.

One type of racing in which the Miata absolutely *couldn't* lose would be a spec series, or a one-marque class allowing only Miatas to run. So far an ongoing Miata spec series is just a dream, although Teddy Yip, the man behind the Macau Grand Prix, did stage one race in 1989. The Teddy Yip Race of Champions consisted of sixteen identical Miatas piloted by such luminaries as Denny Hulme, Innes Ireland, Roy Salvadori, Parnelli Jones, a brace of Unsers, Bobby Rahal, IMSA champ Geoff Brabham and Alan Jones. In the end it was sports car ace Geoff Lees taking the checkered flag after heated battles had wiped out half the field before the finish.

There's also a contingent at Mazda and elsewhere that would like to create some sort of spec series in the States. "God, I'd like to see it happen," muses Mark Jordan. "We could build a series of those Club Racers painted in fluorescent colors. . . . I'd like to see it happen; just something that we could entertain people with, that's what it's all about." Any sponsors listening out there?

But you needn't drain your wallet flying to Macau, or even traveling across America in a fluorescent Club Racer, to compete with your Miata. You don't even have to invest any money in it—the Miata lends itself perfectly to autocrossing, and in autocrossing's Stock classes the car doesn't need any modifications at all to be competitive.

In autocrossing, drivers race against the clock instead of directly against each other. A twisty course is laid out with pylons, usually in a large parking lot, and the driver who gets through it in the least time wins. It's simple, safe and loads of fun. It's also a great way to learn just how far and how fast you can safely push your car.

Getting started in autocrossing is as easy as showing up at an event and getting to know the people involved. Talk to drivers of similar cars—it's likely there will already be more than one Miata around—and ask them what you need to do to get started in Novice racing. Usually, the best plan is to attend one of the SCCA's regional autocross schools, which are held frequently around the country. (The SCCA's own autocross series are called Solo II and Pro Solo.) The Miata Owner's Club of America also has a program to help members get running in autocross and even sponsors some events of its own.

Basically, all you need to put in your Miata to make it competitive in Solo II Stock is gasoline. The rules allow changing the wheels, however, and lighter, slightly wider wheels might help your times a touch. Duane Simpson recommends staying with the stock tire size, though. He's found that wider tires actually slow down the car in an autocross.

Once you get seriously into autocrossing you'll probably want to graduate out of the Stock classes. You can start by looking to aftermarket springs, soft tires and large swaybars to help bring your times down. Simpson has thoughts on Prepared class racing, too: "There are lots of nice kits out there—Rod Millen and Jackson Racing both have a really nice swaybar and spring kit. They've really got them balanced out well." Going with a pre-tested package should save you a lot of unnecessary fooling around.

The real point of autocrossing is having fun, but as in any racing series the professionals can rack up a serious hardware tab. The old racer's adage applies in autocrossing as much as anywhere else: It's better to put money into yourself than your car. If you have to choose between a new set of wheels or a driving school, the school should win out every time.

*Tight, low-speed corners make up a Solo II event, and they're just what the Miata loves most.* **Mazda**

# CHAPTER FIVE

# Miata Aftermarket Equipment

Mazda's designers went to great lengths to make the Miata a statement of individuality. They succeeded so well that sales took off to undreamed-of heights.

Obviously a problem was created that way: How individual can a Miata be if the driver sees another one just like it coming down the road every day? In places like car-crazy southern California, Miata owners are asking themselves that question all the time. (It's not surprising that most companies offering aftermarket goodies for the MX–5 are in or near Los Angeles.) In the same vein, what good are the suspension settings that Mazda knew would be right for ninety percent of the people out there if you find yourself in the other ten percent?

The solution in both cases is to turn to aftermarket equipment: equipment you add to the Miata after Mazda delivers the car. Aftermarket equipment can make your car faster, more attractive or simply different from all the others. The idea is to tailor an individual car to the tastes of its individual owner.

When dealing with aftermarket parts it's important to remember one thing: Mazda's engineers and designers are professionals, and they had very good reasons to build the Miata the way they did. Loading up on aftermarket parts without a clear vision of what you're trying to achieve will probably just give you a less attractive or less behaved car. Done correctly, though, individually tailored Miatas can be great cars indeed.

Mazda knew immediately how popular the Miata would be with the aftermarket and decided to show how nice a specially built example could be. They unveiled their own aftermarket-style car, the Miata Club Sport, at the 1989 Chicago Auto Show. The screaming-yellow Club Sport featured color-keyed Panasport wheels with wide rubber, exposed headlights under plexiglass covers, flared fenders, an elegantly resculpted nose, a fiberglass spoiler and convertible boot, and competition-style exhaust tubing. Inside, the car got luxurious leather upholstery, competition safety harnesses and a leather-wrapped Momo steering wheel. Though Mazda had no plans to market the Club Sport, it did show the potential for a specially prepared MX–5.

One word of caution before running out to build your own Club Sport replica: consult your local dealer to see how any modifications might affect your warranty before you perform them.

## Aftermarket engine

For most people, the Miata's standard 116 horses are more than enough. The car has yet to be built, however, that some owners wouldn't like to be stronger.

Pumping up the Miata's engine is a relatively simple process—the standard B6 block has already proved quite amenable to serious hot rodding in racing and aftermarket street use. It would be easier still for Mazda itself to offer a pumped-up Miata, but don't hold your breath. Rod Bymaster, Mazda Motor of America's manager for sports/sporty cars, says, "That's something that's really just been studied at this point. The main reason is that we have a very favorable insurance rate on this car right now—there's no surcharge for it being a sports car. We're thinking [performance upgrades] may be better left to the aftermarket people." Of course, Bymaster doesn't even have to mention that when something's not broken, you don't go trying to fix it. The Miata's sales are already proving that the engine supplies just the right amount of power for most buyers.

Still, we all know that that little space where the power steering pump fits would be a great place to stick a supercharger. . . .

An engine's performance is dictated by two things: the lesser of them is how much fuel you can shove into a cylinder in a given amount of time; the greater is how much *air*. Since the proper ratio of air to fuel is needed for good combustion, the secret to performance is usually upping the airflow. It's an easy enough matter to squirt a little more gas into the engine, but the only thing forcing air in is standard atmospheric pressure.

*Clean-looking airbox and filter assembly is a visual tip-off to the MazdaSports Fuel Management kit.* **Jackson Racing/MazdaSports**

You can improve the airflow by clearing away as many obstructions from the intake and exhaust tract as possible, and Mazda has already gone a long way toward doing that. Then you can put in new camshafts that perhaps sacrifice a little low-end drivability or economy for the sake of keeping the valves open longer, giving better breathing and higher performance at higher revolutions per minute. But sticking to a normally aspirated engine (one that doesn't use a system to pressurize the incoming air), you can only go so far without incurring tremendous bills. This is particularly true of the already tightly wound MX-5 engine.

One of the best bets to take you that far is a kit offered by MazdaSports, a new arm of Jackson Racing in Huntington Beach, California. The MazdaSports Fuel Management System consists of a new airbox, intake tract, air mass sensor and piggyback computer that, in conjunction with the company's tuned header and exhaust system, MazdaSports claims boosts Miata output by twenty to thirty percent, all for well under $1,500. The idea behind the MazdaSports Fuel Management

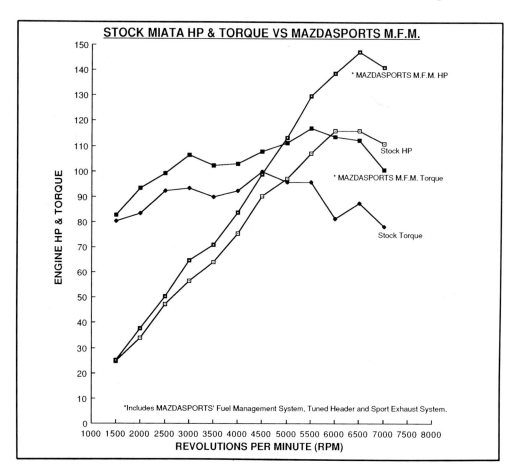

**STOCK MIATA HP & TORQUE VS MAZDASPORTS M.F.M.**

* MAZDASPORTS M.F.M. HP

Stock HP

* MAZDASPORTS M.F.M. Torque

Stock Torque

*Includes MAZDASPORTS' Fuel Management System, Tuned Header and Sport Exhaust System.

ENGINE HP & TORQUE

REVOLUTIONS PER MINUTE (RPM)

*Jackson Racing ran out this computer graph to show performance improvements with their MazdaSports Fuel Management System.*
**Jackson Racing/MazdaSports**

System is primarily to re-route the incoming air away from the hot engine (making it denser) and to replace the stock spring-loaded intake sensor with a less-restrictive Bosch hot-wire air mass sensor.

Rather than measuring the stock spring-loaded sensor's angle and computing airflow from that, the Bosch sensor measures how much current is needed to keep a special wire at a constant temperature as it sits in the intake flow. The hot-wire sensor speaks to the Miata's original intake computer through MazdaSports' piggyback computer. Mazda Motorsports, the manufacturer's official tuning arm, should also have some normally aspirated performance goodies available by the time you read this. Rod Millen Motorsports, of Huntington Beach, California, also has a camshaft and exhaust system kit that dramatically boosts the stock engine's output.

**Turbochargers and superchargers**

Going a step up the performance ladder without a total rebuild requires a *forced induction* system, a turbocharger or supercharger. The idea here is to actually pressurize the incoming charge of air so that more fuel can be stuffed into the engine while still maintaining the proper air-fuel ratio. This means more power—a lot more.

There are two distinct types of forced induction systems, turbochargers and superchargers. Both are basically air pumps. A turbocharger consists of two impellers (fans, if you will) at opposite ends of a common shaft. The first impeller is spun up to 100,000 rpm or more by the blast of escaping exhaust gases, and the second impeller compresses air for the intake system. Turbos are a clever way to get horsepower, because most of the energy that drives them would otherwise be wasted out the exhaust pipe. In theory, you're getting something for nothing; in practice, turbos can have problems, though none of them are insurmountable.

One trouble with turbos is *lag*, a momentary pause between the time the driver steps on the gas and the point at which the turbo speeds up enough to do any good. On a well-built turbo, lag can be almost negligible; on a poorly designed one it can be downright crippling.

Another drawback of turbos is a factor of their own operation—they get hotter than blazes from sticking out in the exhaust flow, and the speed at which they spin compounds the problem greatly through friction. A turbo has to have an ample supply of fresh oil to stay in good shape, and sometimes even needs liquid cooling passages.

The second alternative is superchargers, which are simpler devices with one great drawback. Rather than being driven by exhaust gases, they're mechanically driven by the engine itself. In other words, some of the horsepower they help to create is immediately drained off again to drive the unit itself. Because they're geared right to the engine, though, superchargers aren't subject to lag, and they don't heat up nearly so much as turbos. Currently, the aftermarket scene has been concentrating on turbos, although more than one insider at Mazda has mentioned an interest in supercharging. No doubt Toyota's successful supercharged MR2 has caught their attention.

Two southern California companies are sitting at the top of the turbo Miata heap at the moment, but there will be plenty more entries before the car's day is out. One of them is Performance Techniques in San Bernardino, California, a tuning skunk works under the direction of former aerospace engineer Allan Nimmo. Nimmo had already lined up an impressive list of projects before tackling the Miata, including an RX-7 powered by a 940 hp turbocharged Chevrolet V-8! Nimmo's efforts for the Miata are a little more earthbound than his 200+ mph RX-7, but no less impressive.

The basics of the Performance Techniques turbosystem are a Garrett AiResearch T-2 turbocharger, retimed camshafts and a second fuel management computer to handle the new intake charges. The basic PT package lists for about $3,000, or about $4,500 when installed and tested by Nimmo's crew. Nimmo has also toyed with the idea of a Stage II package including an intercooler—a device to cool the air between the turbo and the engine, giving a denser charge that allows even more fuel to be thrown in the mix. Such a setup would be good for a considerable number of horses on top of the 222 hp PT already claims for the Stage I turbo.

There's no hiding the installed PT turbo (perched next to the cam covers), so make sure your smog papers are in order before your next ticket. **Performance Techniques**

The results of Performance Techniques' tuning speak for themselves. Quarter-mile times fall down into Ferrari Testarossa territory and the top speed climbs above 150 mph. One particularly neat touch to the PT turbo kit is their turbo oiler, a pressurized canister that pumps oil through the turbo for about five

Next page
*Screaming yellow, on the following pages, is almost an official fifth color for southern California Miatas. Millen's elegant turbo installation lives inside this example commissioned by* Road & Track *magazine.* **Guy Spangenberg**

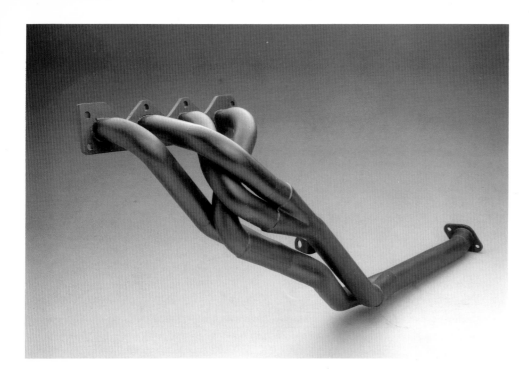

*Lower-restriction exhaust manifold works in concert with the MazdaSports Fuel Management System.* **Jackson Racing/MazdaSports**

minutes after the engine is shut down. The oiler—a universal piece that costs about $100—should go a long way toward extending the life of the blower.

The second big name in the turbo Miata game is Rod Millen, or more accurately Rod Millen Motorsports. Millen, a New Zealander whose shop works out of southern California, was just the man to undertake a hot-rod Miata project. Rod Millen Motorsports has long been tied to Mazda's competition efforts in America, most notably in SCCA PRO Rallying with a special four-wheel-drive RX-7 and later a race-prepped 323 GTX. Millen took the series championships in 1985, 1987, 1988 and 1989.

To simply recap the hardware, the stock Miata engine has been upgraded to a turbocharged unit that Millen estimates is good for 230 bhp—almost double the power of the original. Millen had a head start here, through experience with the similar 1.6 liter dohc Mazda engine in his PRO

Rally champion 323 GTX. The GTX engine donated a turbocharger and intercooler, the almost mandatory lower-compression pistons and a large-capacity radiator. From there Millen added his own low-restriction stainless exhaust system and a second engine-management computer. Finally, his engineers worked overtime to make the installation neat and elegant. From a casual glance at the engine bay, you'd never know that a turbo was hidden under the hood.

Backing up the engine in Rod Millen Motorsports' own fully loaded testbed Miata is a Centerforce clutch and the stock Miata gearbox. Millen's own limited-slip differential resides at the rear of the car. (Millen's limited-slip diff is an especially neat piece if you managed to miss Mazda's own viscous differential option.) Big brakes, racing-grade suspension and some tasteful exterior touches finish off the Millen showcase, running the cost of the whole car up to about $25,000.

Cartech Incorporated, a Dallas-based engineering company famous for RX-7, Honda, Toyota and 5.0 liter Mustang turbo conversions, also has decided to set their sights on the Miata. Cartech shot for long life and a user-friendly power curve rather than overall output. Using a Warner-Ishi RHB-5 turbo with water-cooled bearings and an intercooler, the Cartech system extracts 185 horses and 190 lb-ft of torque from the MX-5's 1.6 liter engine.

## Aftermarket handling

It's also relatively easy to upgrade the Miata's handling. The standard suspension, firm and responsive as it is, is by necessity a compromise between ride and handling—in any car, the softness of the ride falls off as the cornering ability increases. At some point, engineers have to decide where these cross purposes will meet.

The Miata's stock suspension was designed to offer the best

combination of ride, handling and production costs for most of the car's intended buyers. As always, though, there are people more than willing to sacrifice a little ride comfort and money for even sharper handling. Plenty of companies out there are eager to help them.

Most drivers agree that the Miata's stock shocks are excellent, and very often they'll still be there long after extensive retuning of the other suspension bits. Not so the anti-roll bars, however, which are often the first thing to go. It's not that the stock bars are inadequate, it's simply that larger bars immediately reduce body roll (lean) in corners, increasing overall lateral acceleration. (Lateral acceleration is a measurement of the car's resistance to sideways sliding.)

Heavier anti-roll bars also have some downsides as well. They transmit some degree of road noise into the cockpit and stiffen the ride of the car over bumps and tar strips. Anti-roll bars also reduce the independence of the suspension—in other words, they tie the two wheels of an axle together more firmly than they'd be otherwise. The larger the anti-roll bar, the more a jolt to one wheel will affect the other. That's not only uncomfortable, it momentarily detracts from handling. If one wheel hits a bump, the other will experience some degree of movement rather than tracking straight and true down the road.

A car's springs also determine its ride and handling. The softer the spring, the gentler the ride over bumps and dips. Soft springs also mean increased weight transfer (body lean, nose dive and rear squat), however, and don't keep the tires on the road as well as stiff ones.

*Any* springs and bars, then, are a compromise between ride and handling. The stock Miata's suspension settings are pretty stiff, so they're biased more toward handling than ride. Some people feel they just don't go far enough.

Changing springs and anti-roll bars is fine with a specific goal in mind, but just playing with them randomly can get you into trouble. Many people go to stiffer springs and bigger bars in a knee-jerk reaction: If some is good for handling, they think, more is better. That's not necessarily true. Not only do these additions risk making the

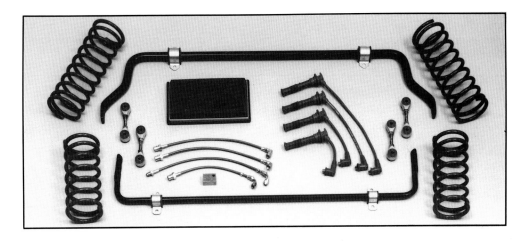

ride too choppy to be comfortable, they can upset the overall balance of the car. The Miata's neutral, predictable handling is a byproduct of what the Japanese call *harmonization:* the perfect integration of springs, anti-roll bars, bushings and so on. Randomly changing one element of the equation can easily give rise to nasty tendencies like oversteer or understeer that will more than cancel out any gain in overall grip.

Often it's best to go to a pre-assembled package for suspension upgrades, and a number are available for the Miata. Companies that offer a complete package had better have done their homework, of course, and that includes plenty of over-the-road testing and skidpad time.

One of the most respected packages comes from Racing Beat of Anaheim, California. Currently, Racing Beat is better known for its line of RX–7 speed accessories, in part because of their responsibility for the

*Springs, anti-roll bars, plug wires, braided-steel brake lines, and air filters form the core of Racing Beat's growing Miata parts list.* **Racing Beat**

*Performance Techniques sets up its own turbo Miata with help from friends at Havasu Racing (wheels) and Eibach North American (springs).* **Performance Techniques**

fastest RX–7s in IMSA competition. But when the Miata came along, it was too good a car to pass up. The company currently offers larger swaybars to be employed with the stiffer and shorter springs they supply, resulting in a Miata with increased road feel, less body roll and more precise steering. (They also offer a custom set of ULTRA racing-type plug wires, a free-flowing air filter assembly and an oil cooler with a remote filter location that's easier to get at than the stock piece.)

From Rod Millen Motorsports comes a set of trick-looking blue powder-coated anti-roll bars for the Miata, 1.00 inch in diameter at the front and 0.75 inch at the rear. Stiffer springs, lowering the car by the same amount front and rear, can be had in the same finish to make a balanced and tested package. MazdaSports, the division of Jackson Racing, also makes

a highly regarded package that's proving its worth in autocrosses around the country.

Of course Mazda Motorsports isn't left out of the picture. For a set of heftier factory-blessed bars and springs you actually need look no farther than your dealer's parts inventory. Other companies are joining the fray as well, and many of them promise to make packages that are just as good as the ones already mentioned. Make sure, though, that any company you buy from has the ability and inclination to thoroughly test their offerings beforehand.

## Aftermarket brakes

Although the Miata's braking system is generally regarded as excellent, drivers who push particularly hard have been known to complain about its level of precision and overall power, particularly on slick pavement. While the stock brakes are usually more than adequate for a Miata, unleashing the kind of power a turbo makes on the car is a pretty good argument for upgrading the brakes as well.

A brake upgrade can be as simple as fitting racing-style pads to fight fade under hard use. (Semi-metallic pads should be available through aftermarket sources by the time you read this.) Another relatively simple addition is fitting braided-steel brake lines, which companies like Racing Beat offer. (Stainless-steel lines offer better brake feel and more leak resistance than the stock rubber pieces.) Some people also prefer silicone brake fluid over the standard item. Silicone brake fluid doesn't absorb water and its boiling point is higher than regular fluid's—unless you start out with silicone fluid, however, you might be asking for trouble. Regular brake fluid causes the rubber in the braking system to swell, which is part of their design, while silicone fluid does not. If the rubber parts have swollen before you switch to silicone, there might be hydraulic troubles down the road.

At the opposite end of the spectrum from minor tweaks like fluid and pads, you can go as far as Rod Millen Motorsports has and revamp the entire brake assembly. For the sum of almost $2,500, Millen offers more brakes than you'll ever need—which is no more than you need in a turbo Miata capable of 150+ mph. Millen's complete brake job consists of transplanting the huge, vented discs from the RX–7 Turbo onto the smaller, lighter Miata. The cost reflects the thoroughness of the Millen package. Not only are specially fabricated brackets and mounting bars included, Millen drills the discs and includes semi-metallic competition brake pads. The results are astonishing: braking distances are reduced by twenty feet from 60 mph and thirty-five feet from 80 mph. Perhaps more importantly, the pedal fade that the stock brakes can experience with hard, repeated use disappears completely.

## Aftermarket wheels and tires

Mazda went to great lengths to design the sport wheels on the Miata; the lower cost pressed-steel jobs were added to the mix strictly for owners who were after the lowest base price possible.

At first, Mazda engineers and stylists worked on a number of wheel designs; eventually conferences between both these groups and manufacturing specialists decided that only one proposal, a Panasport Minilite lookalike, could be made light enough at a cost that wouldn't drive the MX–5's sticker out of sight. The proposed wheel had eight spokes, but it was learned that seven spokes would be lighter, just as strong and better looking, so the seven-spoker was picked for the Miata.

These wheels *aren't* the ultimate on the market, simply the best choice for the average Miata buyer. Some aftermarket wheels are lighter or wider, at least some of the expensive

ones, and all of them will make your Miata look different from the herd.

Lighter wheels benefit the car's ride without sacrificing handling. Consequently, the suspension can be made stiffer and the ride will wind up right back where it started. Wheel weight is extremely important; as part of the *unsprung weight* of the vehicle, the inertia of the wheel traveling up and down determines how much jounce is transmitted to the car itself. Lighter wheels mean less inertia, hence a smoother ride. Remember, though, that the optional sport seven-spokers on the Miata weigh only 12.3 pounds. There are plenty of "lightweight" aftermarket wheels that are actually heavier, and therefore a big step back from Mazda's own equipment.

Another advantage of aftermarket wheels is the ability to fit wider tires. Wider tires, of course, put more rubber on the ground, and that means more overall grip. But with that comes more cost, possibly more noise and often reduced longevity. Wide

*All-white Millen Miata is a guaranteed head-turner.* **Guy Spangenberg**

performance tires usually use softer rubber to aid handling further still, and the softer the rubber, the shorter the tires' overall lifespan. Wider tires also take more muscle to steer, particularly at low speeds, and they reduce the tossability—the ease of initiating a drift—of the car. And, of course, as your tire/wheel combo gets *too* wide, it

sidewall flexing inherent in all tires; they also ride rougher, though, so it's a trade-off.

Experts agree that the Miata is particularly sensitive to *offset*, the distance between a wheel's hub and the center of the wheel. Since most aftermarket wheels don't have the same offset as the stock Miata pieces, many can be ruled out immediately. Current thinking is that the Miata's stock 45 mm offset is ideal, while wheels with 35 to 50 mm of offset will probably fit the bill without too much untoward behavior. Anything more than that should be strenuously avoided.

Among the wheels with matched offset that have already proven successful are the lightweight Havasu Tasac units sold through Havasu Racing, and Rod Millen's special Directional Aero Wheel. Both are costly but perfect matches. Millen also offers up true eight-spoke Panasport Minilites in 14 and 15 inch sizes for the purist, while Fittipaldi and BBS have an assortment of wheels that fit the Miata's needs.

## Aftermarket body and interior

Most owners who uprate the internals of their Miata will want to do at least a little to the exterior to advertise that their car's been given special attention. Often, however, aftermarket externals are put on simply for their own sake—to make an individual car look better, or at least different, than all the rest.

One of the ideas that was kicked around considerably at MANA but discarded before production was a hard boot over the lowered convertible top. Some of these boots were flat, while others had miniature faired headrests ("Like a '63 Thunderbird [Sport Roadster]," says Norman Garrett). The hard boot didn't make it at Mazda, but it seems to be coming on with a vengeance in the aftermarket.

Both flat and faired hard boots

*Semi-faired headrests from Rod Millen Motorsports are the closest you can get to the ones originally proposed by MANA's designers.* Guy Spangenberg

starts to interfere with the body and chassis at full steering lock. Tires up to 205 mm in cross section will fit nicely at the rear, and 195 mm at the front will still leave a touch of room for error.

Rolling diameter—essentially the height of the wheel and tire—also has to be kept very close to the stock 22.8 inches to preserve speedometer accuracy and prevent body interference. That means if you go up to a 15 inch wheel you have to go to a lower aspect-ratio tire: a 50 series instead of the stock 60 series. (The lower the aspect-ratio number the less distance between wheel and tread.) Low-aspect tires handle a touch better because they eliminate some of the can be had from a number of sources now, including most of those already mentioned and some others: Pacific Auto Accessories and Road Show International both offer some nice examples.

One concern with aftermarket body panels like the hard boot is the quality of their fiberglass. The cheaper offerings in the field might have gotten that way by using too little or too cheap a grade of materials, and their longevity could be suspect as a result. For now, though, most seem to be holding together just fine.

Elsewhere on the body, the stock Miata features the most vestigial of rear spoilers. (In fact, the rear lip can't even be called a spoiler as it has no vertical ascension; it looks the part, though, thanks to the cut of the tail panel.) The temptation is great to add a true spoiler to the car, as much for looks as any downforce-adding abilities. Almost all aftermarket suppliers also offer deck spoilers for the Miata, either raised like Racing Beat's or integral like the unit from Pacific Auto Accessories. The choice here is personal, but any Miata deck spoiler shouldn't obscure the center brake light; otherwise, the owner is liable to get ticketed or even rear-ended.

At the front, Mazda has again given the car a vestigial airdam in stock form. That's not enough for some owners, though, who want to make a stronger performance statement or simply modernize the nose of their cars. Airdams have a way of snagging on parking curbs and speed bumps, though, so getting one that's too deep may be asking for trouble.

One of the simplest additions is a bra, like the ones sold by Road Show International and others. The idea behind a bra is that it protects the nose of the car from chips and dings; in point of fact, many bras cause more damage by scraping the paint than they prevent, and all bras will lead to a nose

that fades at a different rate than the exposed body surfaces. Still, if you like the look of a bra, and many people do, it's an easy and inexpensive way to make your Miata stand out from the crowd.

**Personalized Miata equipment**

Personalizing equipment for the Miata is certainly not limited to overt performance or appearance options like engines and spoilers. Just a few of the further options are car covers, steering wheels, seats, interior mats and clothing.

Car covers are a fine idea for keeping the sunshine and dirt off the car, but not so wonderful in rainy or foggy climates. The cheapest covers are usually made of rough material that can scratch paint, so take a few steps upmarket. Whatever you buy, make sure it can breathe—allow water vapors to escape—to keep the finish from getting wet by condensation. One particularly nice option is the Technalon Interior Cover sold by Road Show International, which is custom fit to cover just the top-down interior,

*The PAA deck spoiler recaptures some of the bowed-deck look that Shunji Tanaka removed from MANA's third model.* **Pacific Auto Accessories**

---

Next page

*With a hard boot and deck spoiler on board, on the following pages, 15 inch Panasport wheels and 50 series tires round out a tremendous Rod Millen Motorsports styling package.* **Guy Spangenberg**

sort of like a raised tonneau cover.

Wood or leather steering wheels are an ever-popular item that probably won't find much use on the Miata. An aftermarket steering wheel would mean replacing the stock airbag-equipped unit, which not only prevents the driver from having an airbag in a crash but is a highly dangerous and technical procedure. Airbags are fired by small explosive charges, so unless you have a neighbor in the bomb squad, it's probably best left alone.

If you absolutely must find a place for some wood in the Miata's interior, it's probably better to look to the Mazda Club of America's own cherrywood shift knob, an elegant piece modeled on the Lotus Elan's shifter.

Sport seats like Recaros, Scheels, Corbeaus and Flo-fits may find their way into some Miatas, but the stock seats are so good that they'll probably be more an appearance item than a functional one. Floor mats, on the other hand, are a positive boon to anyone concerned about preserving his or her car's original carpeting. (There had even been some talk of supplying the original Miata with a fully removable floor covering that could be taken out and cleaned.) Look to places like Road Show International and your dealer's option counter for pre-fit mats. The Mazda Finish Line pieces available at your dealer also include niceties like a pre-fit tonneau cover and luggage rack.

To advertise your Miata passion without actually adding anything to your car, you can turn to one of any number of wearable Miata-logoed goodies from Mazda Finish Line, Tech West Accessories and the MCA. These outfits offer shirts, sunglasses, jackets, shorts, sweaters and caps just to name a few. There's even a plastic Miata model kit available from MRC/Tamiya at your local hobby shop, and almost certainly more on the way from the likes of Revell and Monogram.

## Local color: Optional paint schemes

In the beginning, at least, one thing the Miata could really use was a few more colors. The factory red, white and blue paint jobs were nice, but having just the three colors guaranteed seeing lots of other cars that looked just like yours— particularly if you chose the most popular color, red.

More colors were promised for later model years, and silver was the first to appear. But through 1990, at least, the answer for many Miata owners was to repaint their entire cars in a completely different color. The most popular of these seemed to be yellow.

Repainting the Miata is generally a straightforward process, but as with any car a cheap job will give sorry results. It's particularly important to make sure the paint shop you're using is competent and thorough. A lousy paint job will lower the value of your car by considerably more than the money you saved by not going to a reputable business in the first place.

When changing colors, make sure that any shop is prepared to paint not just the external surfaces but hidden areas like the insides of doorjambs and the trunk lid. Make sure also that the shop is equipped to handle the three-material body of the Miata. They'll need to paint the car so that the steel, aluminum and plastic pieces all match and weather at the same rate. The line between a respectable paint job and a botched mess is pretty fine. Ask to see some of the recent work of any paint shop you're considering taking your car to, and if they refuse, get out fast.

As long as you're getting your car painted, you might also want to think about having the wheels done to match. Often, painting all but the outer edge of the wheels gives the nicest effect. The best way to explore

sure there's something on some drawing boards, but we haven't heard anything yet."

Bymaster knew that many major manufacturers were disassembling and studying the Miata as he spoke, but even if they decided to go ahead with MX-5 copycars they'd have a long road ahead of them—and no guarantee of doing as good a job. The structure of Mazda, with its history of cost-sensitive production and internal core of devout car enthusiasts, made it perhaps uniquely suited to build a car like the Miata.

## Collector potential

There's no doubt about it, the Miata will be a collector car—someday. It's important historically, and it's generated loads of good will and enthusiasm while new. Any car that makes so many people smile today will have lots of devotees looking to recapture that feeling some day down the road—and willing to pay for the privilege.

On the other hand, the Miata is anything but rare. Mazda brought about 20,000 1990 models to America, and that number will double in 1991. The robustness of the car should keep a large proportion of them on the road, so there will be a fair amount of competition between sellers when the car finally becomes a collector item.

So, is the Miata a good investment from a strictly financial point of view? Most experts think so, but the question is, under what terms? Will the Miata hold its value in the short term, or would it make more financial sense to let used prices bottom out before looking at the Miata as anything more than entertainment and transportation?

One of the most optimistic soothsayers is Michael Lamm, who stays in touch with the hobby/collector market as a columnist for *Special Interest Autos* magazine. He feels that an argument even for short-term profits can be made. In Lamm's words, he sees "numerous parallels with the VW

Beetle in the mid to late 1950s and even in the early 1960s, when you had to pay more for a used Beetle than the car cost new. There was usually a waiting list for new Beetles of three to six months, and people wouldn't do that; they'd pay more for a used one. I bought a 1958 VW toward the end of that year as practically a year-old car, and I remember paying a couple of hundred dollars more for the car used than it cost new. In fact the only reason I got it at all was because the nurse who had owned it was moving to Saudi Arabia.

"VWs kept their resale value like that through the mid 1960s because the demand stayed very high and the car kept kind of a cult status, as does the Miata. I see a parallel with the Miata because if Mazda doesn't change anything major for a number of years—and there's no reason why they should—then, like the VW, it won't be superseded by a newer model, and the current car will keep its resale value. I'm not sure that the Miata will appreciate a great deal, but it really shouldn't lose its resale value for quite a while—which is something you can't say for most cars."

Much less enthusiastic is Peter Bohr, the author of numerous books and articles on used and classic sports cars, including *Road & Track's Sports Car Classics*. On the Miata as an investment, Bohr explains his views: "In the short term I would definitely say no. The prices are going to come down as soon as the supply starts coming, and I think you're seeing that already. Private individuals who bought them expecting to make a tidy profit, from what I understand they're not. I remember when the Fiat X1/9 came in in 1974 you couldn't get a car and there were waiting lists; then after a year or two the price caught up with demand and it was just like any other used car. Sports cars in general depreciate a lot less than a typical family sedan, so [the Miata] would probably follow a typical sports car depreciation curve."

As for the car's long-term potential, Bohr says: "That's a real crystal balling. It all depends on how long Mazda makes the car without changing it and how many they bring in in the meantime. And I also think you've got this whole collector-car status going on now; I think there are going to be a lot more people squirrelling these things away in garages than squirrelled away, say, an E-Type. For that very reason [the Miata won't appreciate] much in our lifetime."

Somewhere in between is Dave Brownell who, as editor of the collector-car bible *Hemmings Motor News* and an avid collector himself, has always had a special insight on the sports car market. Brownell voices some concerns about interior and paint quality, wondering if problems in that area, should they crop up, will hurt the car's appreciation potential. But, he says, "I imagine mechanically they're just as sturdy as an anvil. As a used car, once Mazda gets up to speed on production, the demand's going to level out and it will experience a large first-year depreciation. In ten years, I would say it would start to become collectible—but I was saying that about the RX-7 and it hasn't happened yet."

He also wonders about the restoration potential for any newer cars: "[The highly collectible Austin-Healey] breaks, but it's fixable. [The Miata] is a very high-tech car for all its alleged simplicity. It's simple in a 1990s sense, but I don't think it's one to squirrel away, I think it's one to enjoy."

Almost everyone agrees, however, that as an investment that's also a car to drive for ten or fifteen years, the Miata should be excellent. Since driving any car costs money, it makes sense to at least buy one that's going to be fun to own and get you *some* of your purchase price back in the end. Proper maintenance will of course be key, because a beat-up or even restored Miata isn't going to be worth nearly as much as one that's been

properly maintained for its entire life. Maintenance should be carried out for other reasons as well, but every bit of day-to-day care can also be seen as an investment.

It's important to realize that the Miata will start to appreciate ten, fifteen or even twenty years down the road, not overnight. A buyer has to be prepared to keep the car at least that long if he or she plans to make money on the other side. Otherwise, he or she would be better off waiting until the 1990 models hit the bottom of their depreciation curve—and that could be quite some time. MGBs, for instance, bottomed out only in about 1987, seven years after the last was made and twenty-five years since the first

one came off the line. Buying an MGB brand new in 1962 as a hedge against inflation would have made for a long wait indeed. It will still be years before such a car reaches its original purchase price when adjusted for inflation.

Big-ticket auctioneers, who many people feel are responsible for the sharp increase in classic car prices through the 1980s, also don't seem to have much opinion of the Miata as yet. Of course, with their hands full of high-cost exotics and up-and-coming sports cars that promise more return per sale right now, the Miata isn't

*A possible* future Miata powerplant lives under the hood of the home-market Mazda Familia Sport 4WD: Mazda's 16 valve, dohc, 1.8 liter four. **Mazda**

going to be their cup of tea for quite a while.

## The future of the Miata

As mentioned in the chapter on aftermarket parts, Rod Bymaster doesn't foresee big mechanical changes for the Miata, at least not in the near future. With a package as successful as the MX–5, Mazda's obviously not going to be changing things in a big hurry. In the engine compartment, for example, it would be possible to shoehorn in Mazda's 1.8 liter four in place of the 1.6—possibly with forced induction. That would require extensive re-engineering, however, and so far very few people have voiced a big desire to see it done.

What *will* be coming up are things like new paint schemes and optional equipment. An automatic transmission has already been announced, as has a new silver finish. "What we'll probably do," Bymaster predicts, "is keep with four colors. There's red, blue, white and the new silver, and we'll probably switch those from time to time." Some possibilities for future colors, he notes, include the British Racing Green that was shown on a Japan-market MX–5 in Tokyo, and "Yellow's always one, or black might be nice to add." But, he stresses, no promises.

Particularly revealing is a little word-association game that Lyn Vogel of the Miata Club of America played out with Bymaster in the first issue of *Miata Magazine* (the official publication of the Miata Club of America):

MCA: Automatic transmission.
Bymaster: Evil necessity.
MCA: Leather interior.
Bymaster: (Pause.) Probably needed.
MCA: Future colors.
Bymaster: Bright, lively.
MCA: Interior colors.
Bymaster: We'd like a tan. Nothing definite yet.
MCA: Hardtop colors.
Bymaster: We understand the need. We're pushing.

MCA: Yearly production numbers.
Bymaster: 40,000.

One other welcome addition that's a good bet to appear as an option soon is ABS, or anti-lock brakes. Anti-lock brakes utilize computer controls to prevent wheel lockup during panic stops. Essentially, sensors at each wheel detect when one is about to lock and the computer releases hydraulic pressure for an instant, allowing all the wheels to rotate at the same rate again. Project Manager Toshihiko Hirai is known to be a big proponent of ABS, and already had a system well under way before the Miata even hit the showrooms.

Since Mazda is reluctant to speak anymore about the possible future of the Miata, journalists have had to make educated guesses on the subject for themselves. The soft front bumper assembly would be relatively inexpensive to change, for instance, so that may be the first thing in the future to be altered. (The Miata Club Sport had such a piece.) It's such a good-looking piece, however, that Mazda could just as easily stay with it forever.

No matter what detail changes might come down the line, the only safe bet in the years to come is that the basic Miata package will be with us for some time. The car's designers speak frequently about shaping the Miata for a ten-year product cycle, and the car's lines seem classic enough to last that long and more.

*Mazda's Club Sport Racer, shown at the 1989 Chicago Auto Show, displayed what could be done with a Miata in the aftermarket. Special nose with deep airdam, flared fenders, deck spoiler, Panasport wheels, and performance exhaust system were just some of the additions Mazda saw fit to make. Most parts were built by Mazda, on the following pages, not the aftermarket, but other suppliers were soon to rush out their own pieces modeled on Mazda's theme.*
**Mazda**

# Specifications

## 1990 Mazda Miata MX-5

### Engine

| | |
|---|---|
| Type | Inline four, belt-driven dual overhead cams, aluminum head and pistons, iron block, ductile cast-iron crankshaft |
| Bore x stroke | 3.1 x 3.3 in. (78.0 x 83.6 mm) |
| Displacement | 97.45 ci (1597 cc) |
| Compression ratio | 9.4:1 |
| Horsepower | 116 SAE net @ 6500 rpm |
| Torque | 100 lb.-ft. @ 5500 rpm |
| Valve gear | Four valves/cyl., fifty degrees included angle, actuated by hydraulic tappets |
| Intake valve dia. | 1.22 in. (31 mm) |
| Exhaust valve dia. | 1.03 in. (26.2 mm) |
| Intake system | Electronic fuel injection |
| Exhaust system | Tubular stainless steel |
| Emissions control system | Single catalytic converter |
| Ignition system | Electronic, breakerless |

### Drivetrain

| | |
|---|---|
| Transmission | Five-speed manual |
| Clutch | Single dry-plate with hydraulic actuation, diaphragm spring |
| Diameter | 7.9 in. (200 mm) |
| Gear ratios | |
| 1st | 3.136 |
| 2nd | 1.888 |
| 3rd | 1.330 |
| 4th | 1.000 |
| 5th | 0.814 |
| Rev. | 3.758 |
| Final-drive ratio | 4.300 |

### Body and chassis

| | |
|---|---|
| Structure | High-tensile steel unibody, monocoque with perimeter subframe, front and rear box-section reinforcements |
| Front suspension | Independent, unequal-length double wishbones, coil springs, cylindrical double-acting shocks, 0.71 in. anti-roll bar |
| Rear suspension | Independent, unequal-length double wishbones, coil springs, cylindrical double-acting shocks, 0.47 in. anti-roll bar |
| Steering | Rack and pinion (power assist optional) |
| Gear ratio | 18.0:1 (15.0:1 with power assist) |

| | |
|---|---|
| **Turns** | |
| Lock to lock | 3.3 (2.8 with power assist) |
| Circles, curb to curb | 30.6 ft. |

### Dimensions

| | |
|---|---|
| Wheelbase | 89.2 in. |
| Length | 155.4 in. |
| Width | 65.9 in. |
| Height (top raised) | 48.2 in. |
| Track | |
| Front | 55.5 in. |
| Rear | 56.2 in. |
| Curb weight | 2,182 lb. |
| Unladen weight distribution | Front, 52 lb.; rear, 48 lb. |

### Brakes, wheels, tires

| | |
|---|---|
| Type | Four-wheel disc, dual-circuit hydraulic actuation with power assist, 8.0 in. vacuum servo booster |
| Discs | |
| Front | 9.3 in., ventilated |
| Rear | 9.1 in., solid |
| Brake swept area | |
| Front | 5.83 sq. in. |
| Rear | 4.1 sq. in. |
| Parking brake | Mechanical on rear wheels |
| Wheel type | Pressed steel (aluminum alloy optional) |
| Wheel size | 5.5JJx14 |
| Tire size | 185/60R14 |

### Performance

| | |
|---|---|
| Acceleration | |
| 0–60 mph | 8.6 sec. |
| ¼ mile | 17.0 sec. at 81.5 mph |
| Lateral | 0.84 g |
| EPA fuel economy rating | 25 mpg city, 30 mpg highway |

### Capacities

| | |
|---|---|
| Coolant system | 1.25 gal. (4.7 liters) |
| Engine oil | 0.95 gal. (3.6 liters) |
| Fuel tank | 11.9 gal. (45 liters) |

### Options

| | |
|---|---|
| Base price (US) | $13,800 |
| Package A: Alloy wheels, leather-wrapped steering wheel, power steering, AM/FM ETR stereo/cassette | 1,145 |
| Package B: Package A plus power windows, cruise control, headrest speakers | 1,730 |
| Viscous limited-slip differential | 250 |
| Air conditioning | 795 |
| Compact disc player | 600 |
| Detachable SMC hardtop | 1,100 |
| Colors: red, blue, white, silver | No cost |

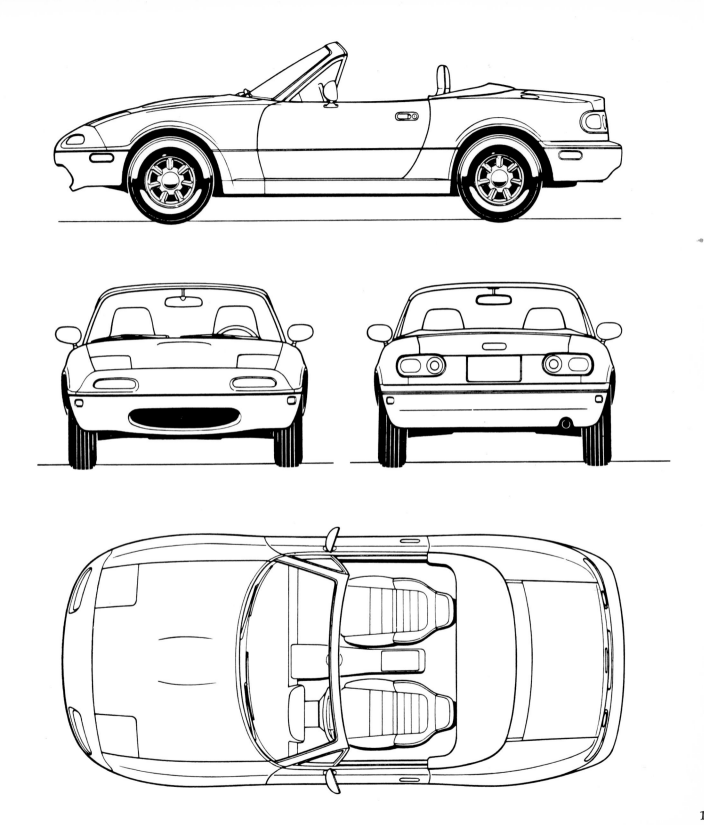

127

# Sources

AAMG Incorporated
4860 San Fernando, Suite 200
Glendale, CA 91205
  Hardtops

Beverly Hills Motor Works
200 S. Robertson
Beverly Hills, CA 90211
  Supplies, cosmetics

Buffalo Bay Trading Company
1301 Carolina St., Suite 107-A
Greensboro, NC 27401
  Miata dress shirts

Cartech Incorporated
11212 Goodnight Ln.
Dallas, TX 75229
  Turbosystems

Cincinnati Microwave
1 Microwave Plaza
Cincinnati, OH 45249
  Escort and Passport radar detectors

Classic Motorbooks
P.O. Box 1
Osceola, WI 54020
  Miata books and literature

Eibach North American
15311 Barranca Pkwy.
Irvine, CA 92718
  Street/competition springs

Havasu Racing
350 10th St.
San Francisco, CA 94103
  Wheels

International Motor Sports Association
P.O. Box 3465
Bridgeport, CT 06605

Mazda Finish Line
(Please contact your
local Mazda dealer)
  Accessories, cosmetics

Mazda Information Bureau
4675 McArthur Ct., Suite 750
Newport Beach, CA 92660
  Mazda press information

Mazda Motorsports
(Please contact your
local Mazda dealer)
  Factory-authorized handling,
performance

MazdaSports/Jackson Racing
16291 Gothard St.
Huntington Beach, CA 92647
  Fuel management systems, handling,
cosmetics

Miata Club of America
5394 Wylstream
Norcross, GA 30093
  Owner and enthusiast services

Miata Club of America
Competition Department
631 Silverleaf
Charlotte, NC 28210

Miata Club of America and *Miata
Magazine*
General Information
P.O. Box 35253
Greensboro, NC 27425-5253

Monarch Mazda
6120 S. Broadway
Littleton, CO 80121
  Cosmetics, headrest speakers, security
systems

MRC/Tamiya
200 Carter Dr.
Edison, NJ 08817
  Miata model car

Pacific Auto Accessories
15241 Transistor Ln.
Huntington Beach, CA 92649
  Cosmetics, hardtop

Performance Techniques
346 S. I St., Suite 3
San Bernardino, CA 92410
  Turbosystems, handling, cosmetics

Racing Beat (Hotchkiss/Associates)
1990 S. Bundy Dr.
Los Angeles, CA 90025
  Handling, cosmetics

Road Show International
293 Pharr Rd.
Atlanta, GA 30305
  Supplies and cosmetics

Rod Millen Motorsports
7522 Slater Ave. #122
Huntington Beach, CA 92647
  Turbosystems, handling, cosmetics,
wheels

Simpson Brothers Racing
631 Silverleaf
Charlotte, NC 28210

Sports Car Club of America
9033 E. Easter Pl.
Englewood, CO 80112
  Competition organization

Tech West Accessories
P.O. Box 52683
Livonia, MI 48152
  Clothing

The Tire Rack
3300 W. Sample
South Bend, IN 46619
  Tires, wheels

Winner International
Winner Bldg.
Sharon, PA 16146
  Mechanical security systems

WRC/Revolution Wheels
1464 Makefield Rd.
Yardley, PA 19067
  Wheels